C000082586

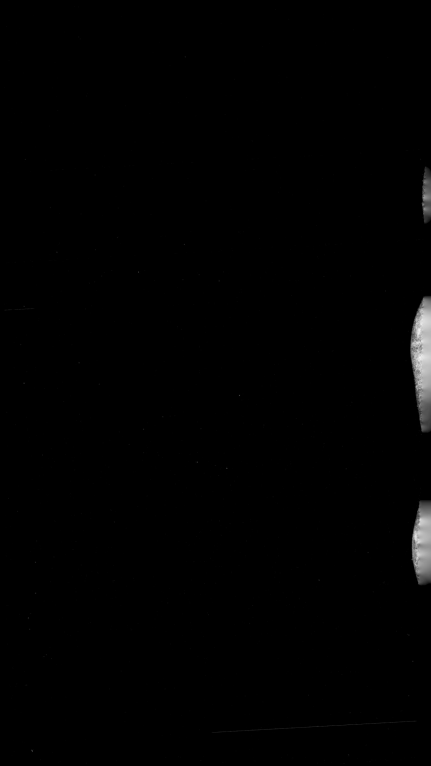

I dedicate this book to Samantha, because if you hadn't sent that text wanting a chat over a cup of tea, we would never have gone on this epic journey together.
Thank you.

Naomi

I dedicate this book to Naomi – none of it would have been created without you. Who would have thought that the chance meeting on July 28th, 2017, would have led us on such an exciting journey – one that I would not want to be on with anyone else.
Thank you.

Samantha

Dearest Di,
May this book make you laugh, cry, grow, question, answer and become an even more beautiful version of you.
Hoping the same for Isla, too.
With love,
Sam
xxx

Naomi Sharp has self-published six books: two adult personal development books and four of twelve YA fiction books which are part of a series called the Universal Series. Naomi has an Equine Assisted Therapy Centre and works with children with mental and physical disabilities, and emotional imbalances. She is a true country girl at heart.

Samantha Bell has over twenty-five years' experience guiding and teaching children and parents. She has worked with all ages, in various sectors, including a school for children with emotional and behavioural difficulties and behavioural therapy. She currently manages an incredibly successful baby and child sleep consultancy.

Naomi Sharp & Samantha Bell

RAISING A WARRIOR

An all-in-one, no-nonsense guide
for children and adults

AUSTIN MACAULEY PUBLISHERS™

LONDON • CAMBRIDGE • NEW YORK • SHARJAH

A CIP catalogue record for this title is available from the British Library.

ISBN 9781528940009 (Paperback)
ISBN 9781528940016 (Hardback)
ISBN 9781528970174 (ePub e-book)

www.austinmacauley.com

First Published (2019)
Austin Macauley Publishers Ltd
25 Canada Square
Canary Wharf
London
E14 5LQ

Contents

Introduction

RAISING A WARRIOR: The Trilogy

Raising a Warrior is, fundamentally, a guide for adults. But it's a journey that adults and children can actively take together. It focuses on no-nonsense, step-by-step guidance, but also heavily involves the children themselves, by encouraging them to proactively engage in self-led, creative activities. It's all prompted by and built on the platform of an inspiring novel. *Raising a Warrior* brings adults and children together, and the teaching and learning is nurtured through both individual and joint action.

It will appeal to those who want to be actively involved in children's development, but who are also conscious of children taking charge of their own.

This unique, three-book project has been created to facilitate family/group-time, childhood reading, and fun and open communication, as together, you explore great ideas and thoughts through the power of a thought-provoking story.

HOW TO USE THE TRILOGY

Part 1: The novel, Lucy and Sarah is the starting point and facilitator to the project as a whole. It has been written to introduce specific lessons and principles, and will also act as an opener to conversations between you and your children – especially the tough ones. Lucy and Sarah will take the readers on the journey of two sisters who have faced the most unimaginable tragedy of losing their parents, but must now tackle separation from each other. They must walk away from the only life they have ever known, towards a future yet to be written. Even though their paths lead them miles from each other, their journeys continue to intertwine in a sometimes challenging, yet wondrous way. Along the way, they each learn wisdom from life and new friends, discover hidden strengths, hope and opportunities, and heal their broken hearts. The readers will follow their story as they find the courage to make brave, new choices, and create the life of their dreams.

You can read Lucy and Sarah together, or not – we don't mind. Your children may want to read it on their own. This is OK. But, we do feel you will be able to guide them better if you read it in your own time as well.

Part 2: The Activity Book will guide the children through twenty activities. Each one is designed to teach them how to tackle personal challenges with confidence and self-assuredness, and follow their dreams. It has been written through the voices of Lucy and Sarah, to better teach the children these valuable life lessons, through practical and creative means. The activities will also inspire them to dream big, speak up, be themselves…and yes, get outside!

You don't need to read all twenty activities in one go. Simply go through, one activity at a time, at a pace that suits you. When you're ready, you can read the activities alone, with your child, or perhaps you can ask your children to read a specific activity out loud to you.

Don't worry if your children choose to do some of the activities with their friends, somebody else or even alone. This is their choice. We still recommend keeping up to speed with all the activities though…just in case.

If you are a parent, you will be able to carry out all of the activities directly with your child. If you are guiding/caring for a child in a different setting, you may only be able to focus on the planning stages of a few of the activities. This may mean that your child will have to implement them at home, without you, but that's OK. Simply choose the approach that works best for you and which maximises your child's learning from that particular activity.

Oh, and PLEASE feel free to adapt and 'tweak' any or all of the activities, if you like. After all, you know the children in your care, and what appeals to them, specifically.

Part 3: The Adult's Guide will break each of the activities down for you and highlight the life principles and values they are aiming to teach, and the motives behind each one. You will be given practical suggestions about how to pass on key life-skills, handle adversity, and teach gratitude and kindness. It will steer you through the challenges you may face as you navigate meltdowns, conflicts and tricky conversations. It will offer practical, step-by-step advice for many different aspects of raising/guiding/educating a child within this age range. Adults in a non-parent role can use the three-book project directly with the children they are caring for and/or as a teaching resource with the parents they are working alongside.

Trigger questions: With each activity, we have provided you with Trigger Questions. These are for you to use when you feel you need to open up the conversation rather than steer it. You will notice that each Trigger Question is open-ended. This will create the space to allow your children to seek the answers for themselves.

The Adult's Guide is laid out in roughly the same format as the Activity Book, which have been designed to use alongside each other. So, when your little bundles of energy keep pestering you about one of the twenty activities, you will be better equipped and ready to answer the 1001 questions that may be coming your way.

***

Key Words: For simplicity, throughout this guide, we will mostly refer to you as 'adult'. Please note though that this includes adults in all different types of caring role, e.g. biological parent, foster parent, grandparent, key worker, nanny, mentor. Also, no matter who you are, for ease, we will refer to the children as 'your' children throughout the guide.

By the way, we are not concerned if you or your children understand the intricacies of child psychology and childhood development. We are more concerned with doing, being and taking action. We feel that learning through proactivity helps people to BECOME their favourite philosophies and lessons. Now that is teaching at its best.

Every bit of guidance in Raising A Warrior is based on real-life experiences with the families we have been lucky enough to guide and teach, and the professionals we have had the pleasure of working with.
Thank you.

Naomi and Samantha

Part 1
Lucy and Sarah

Contents

Hope

"Ring-a-ring o' roses,
A pocket full of PONIES,
A-tishoo! A-tishoo!
We all fall down!"

"It's not 'PONIES', it's 'POSIES'," giggled Lucy as she playfully rolled her eyes at Sarah. But she knew it was pointless asking her little sister to sing the correct words to their long-loved song. Sarah looked up from the game she had been playing with her beloved toy horse, Dandelion. Sunlight streamed through the attic window, cascading a pool of light onto the wooden flooring. Minute dust particles hung, suspended in the light, like tiny fairies waiting for something, perhaps.

"What are you doing, Lucy?" Sarah asked, with wary curiosity. Lucy was seated by their box, playing, as always, with her two dolls, who were impressively dressed in some of Lucy's latest design-creations. Sarah unfolded herself from her cross-legged position, picked up Dandelion-Horse, edged her way across to Lucy and sat down by her big sister's side. Lucy paused, looked purposefully from the dolls to Sarah and declared theatrically, "They are finally getting married!"

Sarah tilted her head in confusion. "What's married?" she asked. Lucy tutted dramatically, got to her feet and stepped purposefully onto the top of their box. She held the dolls majestically out in front of her. "It's when a man and a lady promise to love each other for ever and ever and ever, and live together and have lots of babies and be in love and hold hands every day, and the man will promise to bring the lady flowers and give her lots of kisses."

Sarah put two fingers into her mouth, wrinkled her little button-nose and pretended to be sick!

"Yuk, that's disgusting," she spluttered through fake retching noises. She picked up Dandelion-Horse, gave him a reassuring kiss on the nose and held him protectively to her. Lucy jumped off the box with a thud!

"All right then, smarty-pants, what do you think married is?" At this, Sarah leapt up onto their chest and held her horse-friend above her head.

"I think married is when a man and a lady live together and he shouts at her and she shouts at him and they never smile and he slams doors and she is always crying and he is always just telling her what to do and she just has to do it!" Sarah slid down off the box, suddenly disheartened. Lucy looked at her in shock.

Lucy placed her hands crossly on her hips. "That's just silly, Sarah!"

"No, it's not!" Sarah shot back in frustration.

"Well," said Lucy haughtily, "that's what my dolls are doing and that's what I am going to do when I am bigger! I am going to get married and wear the biggest, sparkliest white dress, and my husband is going to be the most handsome man in the whole wide world!"

"That's just yucky, Lucy!" sniffled Sarah in response. "I am going to have loads of my very own ponies and lots and lots of other animals too! I don't want a smelly man!"

Lucy slumped down heavily next to their wooden box and slowly traced the grooved outline of their names with her finger. But as she lifted the lid, her irritation lifted with it. The familiar creak of the hinge seemed to squeak, 'peace, please'. She peered inside the box as Sarah knelt by her sister's side, once again. The argument was forgotten…for that moment, at least.

Lucy took a deep breath and looked, wide-eyed, into the box, a small smile starting to curl the corner of her mouth. "Do you remember when Mummy gave us this box?" she asked. Sarah started to feel a little calmer too and willingly joined Lucy on this well-worn trip down memory lane.

"Yes, why?"

Lucy looked at Sarah, her eyes shining. "We named it the, 'What-I-Want-To-Be-When-I-Grow-Up-Box'. Do you remember?"

Sarah grinned and nodded her head.

Lucy reached into the box, just as she had done many times before. "Look," she said with a familiar feeling of excitement. She pulled out a dried flower saved from their parent's wedding day, a tiny white, leather purse which had held her mum's wedding ring and the book of Cinderella. She placed them all gently on the floor. "That's what I want when I grow up," she breathed dreamily as she gazed at her precious treasures.

Sarah dismissed them with a casual wave of her hand. Instead, she reached into the box and took out her book of cowboys and Indians. "Yeah," she retorted, "but this is for real life!" She placed her book squarely on top of Lucy's, before reaching back in and grasping her toy cow and toy sheep.

Lucy shook her head, completely baffled. "You can't marry them!"

"Why not?" Sarah asked with a cheeky smirk. "I love them, and isn't that what you said married is?" Lucy pushed Sarah's book away and flipped open her fairy-tale story.

"No, silly! This is what marriage is meant to be." And she pointed determinedly to Cinderella and her Prince Charming, gliding around the ballroom.

Sarah scooped up her animals with a sulky 'hmmph'. "Well, I'm not getting married, if that's what it is! I just want my animals when I grow up and I can do what I want!"

Sarah stomped off to the other side of the room and began to play with her animals, alone. She reached for an old cardboard box, turned it onto its side and cleverly created an instant toy-barn for her best friends. Lucy remained where she was and became lost, once again, in her book. "But this is real life too," she whispered, as she closed her eyes to better absorb her daydream.

The mood in the attic was suddenly broken by a shout from downstairs. "Girls! Your dinner's ready! Come and wash your hands!" It was their mum, Penny, calling them. Lucy and Sarah both dropped what they were doing and bounded downstairs; little elephants creating mini-earthquakes on each step! They raced into the kitchen, pushing each other aside in a bid to be the first to reach the tap.

"Now, girls, take your time," said Penny as she skilfully sidestepped them. It was a well-practiced manoeuvre! Penny placed both her and her husband's plate on the table. "Mmmm! Thank you, love, this smells delicious," smiled George as he breathed in the rich aromas.

Sarah cupped her hands under the tap to collect a pool of water. A look of mischief crossed her face as she swiftly flicked the water at Lucy! "Hey! No fair," complained Lucy. Sarah quickly darted to her place at the table with an innocent, 'who me?' flutter of her eyelashes.

"Mum, tell her!" whined Lucy.

Penny brought the last two plates to the table. "Come and sit down now, Lucy. Dinner is ready," she replied. Penny shot Sarah a swift but stern look, which caused Sarah to look down guiltily at her hands. Well, almost guiltily. Lucy dried her hands and rudely stuck her tongue out at Sarah as she joined her family at the table. Just a typical dinnertime at the Roberts' house!

George repositioned himself in his chair and placed his hands down on the table. "You know the drill, girls. Who is going to start by telling us one thing you are thankful for today?" Sarah and Lucy glanced quickly across at each other and then promptly down at their plates.

"I'll begin then," said Penny, breaking the silence. "I am thankful for someone sharing their car park ticket with me today because they hadn't used up all their time."

Lucy suddenly looked up, enlightened! "I am thankful today for my notebook!"

"And why is that?" asked George in amusement.

"So I can start to write my present list for my fourteenth birthday!" Everyone erupted into laughter.

"Typical Lucy," responded Penny, shaking her head lovingly at her eldest daughter.

Sarah then began to shout: "I am thankful for playing outside longer at break-time because we all finished our work for Miss and I could make mud pies with Sally!"

Penny leant back in her chair and smiled at Sarah. "And do you want to tell Daddy what happened next?"

"No," said Sarah as her cheeks began to burn. Penny chuckled at Sarah's obvious attempt to now avoid all eye contact with her dad. Penny continued. "Didn't Miss have to give you and Sally spare clothes from the 'Lost and Found' because you were covered, head to toe, in mud?!"

Sarah slowly began to grin. "Maybe," she muttered as she swung her legs playfully underneath the table.

At this, Lucy lifted up her arm and wafted her finger towards Sarah. "Sarah and Sally in trouble again, in trouble again, in trouble again," she sang tauntingly.

"No, we weren't! Shut up, Lucy," Sarah whined, and promptly kicked her sister under the table.

"Ow! That really hurt! God, eight year olds are so annoying," Lucy said as she rubbed her shin.

George firmly interrupted with what the girls called his 'I Mean Business' voice. "We'll have none of that, Sarah. That's unacceptable behaviour. Now, moving on – I am thankful for us all being here now, together, despite me being outnumbered by you women." George playfully tutted and breathed an exaggerated sigh, but everybody knew he wouldn't have it any other way.

"So, were you girls playing with that box again?" asked Penny as she took the first mouthful of her famous shepherd's pie.

Sarah was quick to answer. "Yeah, but Mum, Lucy said that I had to get married and kiss smelly boys and live with them and hold their hands!" Her face crumpled into a look of disgust for the second time that day.

"No, I didn't," Lucy shot back. "She asked what married was and so I told her."

She folded her arms firmly across her chest.

"Please don't make me marry someone, Mum," cried Sarah. "I just want my animals! I don't want to have a stupid husband!" She began to shovel forkfuls of her shepherd's pie unhappily into her mouth.

"Slow down, Sarah!" interrupted George. "We don't want you eating the plate as well!"

Penny hesitated for a moment. "Sarah, why don't you want to get married, love?" she asked with interest. Sarah paused with her fork in mid-air and her mouth open wide. "Because men just shout all the time and tell ladies what to do!"

"OK," said Penny kindly. "Have you ever heard me and your dad shouting and telling each other what to do?"

"Well, no," said Sarah hesitantly, as she began to push her food awkwardly around her plate.

"So where did you get that idea from, sweetheart?" Penny asked, gently trying to coax some more information out of her youngest. Sarah set down her knife and fork and turned to Penny with a frown.

"Mu-um," she said impatiently. "I dreamt it of course! It's obvious isn't it?"

Penny motioned for Sarah to continue and she was only too happy to oblige. "In my dream I was like Pocahontas but I wasn't actually Pocahontas, and my daddy was the big chief and he told me to marry this cowboy man and I never saw my family again, and the cowboy man just told me what to do and shouted at me every day and I couldn't speak and I always had to stay quiet, and then he rode on his horse and was really nasty to it!" Sarah visibly shivered at her dream-memory as Penny and George both exchanged a knowing glance.

"That was just a dream, silly," said Lucy. "Dreams aren't real. I mean, last night I dreamt I was a queen and my husband was the king and we lived in a big castle and we had pink mermaids swimming in our castle moat! Are you telling me that's real?" she enquired sarcastically. Suddenly, George's chair-legs squeaked across the tiles of the kitchen floor, silencing the girls. He leant back in his chair and intertwined his fingers in his lap. He looked directly at Lucy. "So, you want a husband?" he asked, before shifting his gaze to Sarah. "And you want lots of animals? Is it possible," he questioned wisely, "that it's OK to want different things when you grow up?"

Sarah and Lucy both stopped for a moment as they pondered George's questions.

"But, how can she not want to get married?!" Lucy asked wide-eyed as her arms flailed in utter disbelief. George looked down and he shifted his feet. A quizzical smile started to spread across his lips.

"Now, Lucy, what would the world look like if we all wanted to grow up to be and have the same things?" he asked. Lucy lowered her arms as she contemplated the thought, with just a little more curiosity this time.

Penny began to collect the plates. "Think about your dream wedding, Lucy. Who would do your flowers and who would take the photographs if all anybody wanted to be was a wedding-dress designer?" She left the intriguing question hanging in the air as she made her way across to the dishwasher with the dirty crockery. George glanced at Sarah. "Could you be a darling and go and fetch the red book that's on the little table, next to my reading chair? Thanks, poppet."

Sarah slid off her chair and galloped happily to the living room to collect the book. "Now, come here, Miss Lucy." He patted his knee in invitation. Lucy pushed back her chair with a grin. As she reached George's side, he wrapped his left arm around her and scooped her up onto his lap. Sarah trotted back into the kitchen and George deftly caught her too, and bundled her up onto his other knee.

As he wrapped his arms around his girls in a bubble of love, he reached for the book. He opened it up and turned to a specific page. "I want to teach you about the Aborigines."

Sarah looked up, confused. "The 'Abba' what 'knees'?" she asked.

Penny chuckled as she efficiently rinsed and cleared their dinner debris. George looked across at Penny's smile and winked before continuing.

"Well, one group of Aborigines are from Australia. They were the very first people to live there. Some of them live in a place called The Outback where there are no buildings or cars, schools or television."

"No television?!" shrieked Lucy.

"I know," said George in fake shock as he placed the back of his hand melodramatically on his forehead. "Hard to imagine isn't it?" he added with a glint in his eye. "But part of their culture is to live together with just the plants and the animals, and the earth. Obviously they need to eat, drink and keep warm, and they need medicine when they get sick, just like we do. But, instead of everybody in the tribe having the same dream or being given the same job, each person discovers what they love to do and what they are good at. And that then becomes their role within the family. The tribe then has a hunter, a water-finder, a fire builder and a medicine-plant picker, rather than just a whole family of fire-builders. So, girls, there is room in this world for you, Lucy, to be an adoring wife and for you, Sarah, to have lots of animals, if that is what you both want."

Penny dried her hands and took her seat back at the table. "It's important to remember, girls, that your dreams are *your* dreams and to hold tight and listen to them. It's also important to believe that there is always a path that will get you there. You just need to have courage to sometimes do things that you may feel are a bit scary. But, this will help you become the person you need to be in order to make those dreams come true."

"You mean like the Scarecrow in *The Wizard of Oz?*" asked Sarah.

"Exactly," answered Penny. "And remember, there are all sorts of reasons why people have different dreams. But if a person has a different dream to yours, it doesn't make them wrong or 'silly'. Their dream is just as special to them as yours is to you, even though you may not understand it, or even like it."

The girls looked slightly perplexed, so Penny continued. "You see, girls, if we follow our own dreams, it means we all then have something to offer to the world. Something different but something special. And we can then all become a big Aboriginal tribe," she concluded. Lucy and Sarah looked at Penny, still a little blank. "All right," said Penny thoughtfully. "Imagine the world is like a giant shepherd's pie and all the people in the world are the ingredients. In the beginning the ingredients are separate, but if you put them all together, you create something whole and delicious. But, it wouldn't be the same or perhaps quite as delicious if even one of those ingredients was missing. They are all essential."

The girls both started to nod in slow understanding. "I would be the mashed potato," Sarah giggled. "Nice and messy!"

"And I would be the oven that cooked it all," added Lucy.

"I would be the garlic, surely," chuckled George. "Because aren't boys supposed to be smelly, Sarah?" he asked cheekily. He placed the book down on the table and began to tickle both his girls. They squirmed on his lap in fits of giggles, both delighted that Dad-School was now closed.

As Sarah and Lucy managed to escape from George's Mr Tickle fingers, Penny took hold of each of their hands. "Don't forget, girls, 'HOPE' is the feeling that will help you to believe that you can be or do or have anything you want. But you must hold tight to that belief in yourself. It's more than OK to hope for something to come true. And it's definitely OK to believe that it *will* come true, even when it is a baby-dream only just starting to take shape in your head."

Loss

"But who is going to take the box?" whispered Sarah pitifully, her voice just a small, sad sound. She and Lucy were squeezed as far as they possibly could be into the darkest corner of the attic. There was no sunlight streaming through the window today. There were no hopeful fairies.

Lucy looked down at her baby sister's tear-stained cheeks and terrified saucer-eyes. She pulled her into her arms and rocked her back and forth. "It's going to be all right," she soothed, and hoped her words would drown out the sound of her heart breaking into a thousand pieces.

They both suddenly turned to each other in alarm as they heard the doorbell. The cheery chime sounded harsh and mocking. Lucy stood first and reached her hand out to Sarah. "OK. Here we go. Hold on to me," she said, with more bravery than she felt.

"Can't we just stay here forever?" pleaded Sarah.

"You know we can't," Lucy answered gravely. Her legs felt unbearably heavy as she walked each impossible step towards the attic door. She peered over her shoulder at Sarah dragging reluctantly behind. She seemed so tiny.

They slowly entered the kitchen to be greeted by their Grandma Roberts. She had already answered the door and let their unwelcome visitor in, and was busy making tea, but her movements looked forced and uncomfortable. "Can you sit down for me please, girls?" asked Grandma Roberts. The sisters walked over to George's place at the kitchen table and squashed themselves into his chair, together. They clasped each other's hands tightly as Sarah nestled into Lucy's shoulder.

"You remember Mrs Grey, don't you, girls?" asked Grandma Roberts, as she gestured towards their guest. "She is the nice lady who has helped us arrange where you are both going to live now."

The sisters looked down at their hands. The only sign that they had heard the question was a barely noticeable nod from Lucy.

Mrs Grey awkwardly cleared her throat. "Hello, girls," she said in a too-loud voice. "Do you remember why I am here today?"

Lucy nodded again, but Sarah suddenly glared at Mrs Grey and frantically shook her head. "Go away, go away, go away!" she cried desperately. Lucy pulled her closer.

"Come on now, little Sarah," soothed Grandma Roberts. "We've spoken about this lots of times, for months and months now, love. You know that Mummy and Daddy didn't survive the accident, and that they aren't coming back, and that you can't stay here." Grandma Roberts and Mrs Grey looked helplessly at each other, at a complete loss. The pain seemed forever etched into their faces.

"And I've told you for months and months that they haven't totally disappeared!" shouted Sarah. "They did survive! They did! They've just gone back to live in the stars, that's all! I saw their stars again last night! They can still see me and I can still see them!" The tears returned with greater urgency and streamed down her cheeks; little waterfalls of misery. She angrily wiped at her eyes with her sleeve. "I honestly saw them again last night! I did, I did! You have to believe me!" she added forcefully.

"Well, anyway! My teacher said it's completely OK to think that way if I want to!" Lucy tightened her grip even more on her little sister.

Mrs Grey knew there was nothing she could say to calm the frightened girl before her, so made the heart-wrenching decision to proceed with what needed to be done. "I think you remember the last time I was here, girls?" she enquired. "It was a few months ago?" There was no response so she continued: "We talked about where you are going to live now that your mum and dad have...um...well, now that they have...err, you know...gone back to live in the...err...stars?" She looked hopefully at Sarah. Still no response. Mrs Grey self-consciously tucked a stray strand of hair over her ear and turned instead to Lucy. "You know that you are going to Bath, to live with your Grandma Roberts?" she enquired uncomfortably. "And Sarah, dear, you know that you are going to live with your godmother, Aunt Lily, on her farm up in Scotland?"

Sarah jumped to her feet and banged her fists furiously down on the kitchen table. "Why can't we go together?!" she yelled.

Grandma Roberts lifted up her cup of tea and carefully wiped away the resulting spillage. "We've talked about this before, sweetheart," she said wearily. "I am too old to take care of both of you, and your godmother, Aunt Lily, promised to look after you if anything ever happened to your mummy and daddy."

Sarah stormed out of the room and raced back up the stairs. She sat on top of her and Lucy's box and her little body sobbed and shook.

Lucy edged her chair closer to the kitchen table and placed her hands in front of her. She intertwined her fingers, just like she had seen her daddy do many times before. She calmly looked at Mrs Grey. "Yes, Mrs Grey, we understand. When is Lily coming to collect Sarah?"

Mrs Grey readjusted her pleated, beige skirt, trying, unsuccessfully, to put off the inevitable. "She will be here any minute. We didn't want to delay this. We thought that would be better for everybody." Lucy sat completely still.

"OK, I'll go and tell Sarah," she said mechanically. She turned slowly to her grandma. "Are we also going today?" she asked.

Grandma Roberts took a shaky mouthful of tea. "Yes, my love, as soon as Sarah has left."

Lucy got up from the chair and slowly brushed some imaginary crumbs off her jeans. She took a deep, calming breath, squared her shoulders and quietly made her way back up to the attic.

Grandma Roberts turned to Mrs Grey. "As you can see," she said with a sigh. "They're both dealing with this in very different ways."

"That's OK," replied Mrs Grey levelly. "They each need to express their feelings in their own way."

Upstairs, Lucy found Sarah, still sitting on their box, gazing blankly out of the window, at nothing. "You take our box," instructed Lucy decisively. "I'll carry it downstairs for you and put it with your bags. Lily will be here soon to pick you up, so I think you should go and put your shoes and coat on now."

25

"I *will* take it," snapped Sarah sulkily. "I think it should be mine and not yours. I want it and I don't think you should have it!" she added sullenly. Lucy had no intention of arguing with her.

Sarah continued to sit on their box, but all the fight and hope suddenly drained from her body. Lucy took Sarah's hand and gently brought her attention back into the room. She tried to guide her little sister off the chest but Sarah clung on to what was now her life-raft, in one last desperate attempt. "Please, Lucy! Can't we stay here together? I don't want to live with Aunt Lily! This is our house! Please, Lucy!" she begged desperately.

Lucy pulled at Sarah, a little more insistently this time. "Come on, Sarah. We have to do this." She quickly lifted up their box before Sarah had chance to reclaim her seat there. She turned and began to make her way, once more, to the top of the stairs. Sarah held on tightly to the back of Lucy's jumper as she followed miserably in her big sister's footsteps. They both flinched at the sound of the front door opening and the ensuing, hushed conversation between Aunt Lily and Grandma Roberts. The sisters bravely continued their journey down the stairs and into the hallway. Their packed bags stood by the front door, like guards on duty, alert to danger and threat.

As the girls approached, Lily quickly turned her head in the other direction. She hastily wiped away a single tear with the back of her hand. It had been attempting a daring escape for the last hour of her journey and she had no intention of letting it win now or, more importantly, letting the girls see. Lily glanced guiltily at Grandma Roberts with a tiny, helpless shrug. She managed to squeak, "Hi, girls," but her voice sounded strained and unnatural. She looked uneasily about her. Mercifully, the awaiting bags provided a welcome distraction from this impossibly tragic situation. As Lily busied herself with taking Sarah's cases outside to her truck, Lucy followed behind with their beloved box. Sarah urgently ran to Grandma Robert's side. Surely it was worth one last try. "Grandma Roberts, I promise I will behave and be a good girl. I won't be any trouble. Just let me come with you and Lucy!" she begged unhappily.

Grandma Roberts reached down and embraced her lost, little Sarah. "My love, your life is going to be so wonderful up there on the farm. You are going to have so much more fun with your

Aunt Lily and her animals. And they need a special girl like you there to help look after them all."

Sarah suddenly felt a hand on her shoulder. Afraid, she turned to find Aunt Lily and Mrs Grey behind her. "It's time to go, Sarah," said Lily. "If we head off now we'll beat the rush hour and be back for tea. We may even have time to do the evening checks on the farm," she added desperately as she tried to swallow down her own fear and grief. She forced her mouth into what she hoped resembled a reassuring smile.

Lucy hardened her face, pulled Sarah coolly into a quick hug, pushed her back and glanced down at the floor. "I'll, err, call you as soon as I can," she said without emotion. She stepped back and stuffed her hands deep into the pockets of her jeans.

Sarah looked bewildered. "Why are you being weird with me, Lucy?" she questioned with big, sad eyes, but Lucy remained silent. The moment had arrived. There wasn't an attic big enough to hide in now.

Lily took Sarah's hand and led her through the front door of her life-long home and out to the awaiting truck. She opened the passenger door and Sarah clambered into the seat. Lily glanced back at the house as she closed the truck door behind her. She went around to the driver's side, climbed in and slammed her door shut too, flinching at the mechanical 'clang'. Sarah stared sorrowfully out of the rear window at Grandma Roberts and Lucy, who had made their way to the front porch step. Grandma Roberts raised her hand to wave goodbye and prayed with all her might that she would be able to hold her tense smile in place, for just a few minutes longer. Lucy did not look at the truck. Instead, she studied some imaginary stones that she was kicking with her feet. But she did hear the truck come to life, and she did hear it pulling out of the drive, and she did hear the engine gradually fade to nothing, taking her baby sister with it. The silence was deafening.

***

"This truck smells disgusting! It's like poo!" said Sarah, wrinkling her nose as she turned to face the front. "It makes me want to be sick! I bet Grandma Roberts' house doesn't smell!"

she added rudely. She folded her arms determinedly across her little chest.

"That's the farm smell, Sarah," said Lily. "It's from all the different animals. You'll get used to it, and it won't seem so bad in a few days," she explained cheerily, trying urgently to lighten the mood. "I've bought you a present," Lily continued optimistically. "You'll need these on the farm." She carefully reached behind the passenger seat to retrieve a pair of purple, spotty wellies, and handed them to Sarah.

"I don't want your stupid wellies or any presents from you!" retorted Sarah miserably. "I want to go to Grandma Roberts's house with Lucy! I don't want to live with you," she added, and threw the wellies, hard, at Lily.

Lily tightened her grip on the steering wheel and took a deep breath. "Sarah, I understand that you are upset, and it's OK for you to be angry, it really is, but you can't do things like that whilst I'm driving, or we could be in an accident, like your mummy and daddy."

Sarah suddenly put her fingers in her ears. "I can't hear you! La-la-la-la-la-la," she sang dismissively, and turned curtly to face her window. A heavy air of awkward silence descended on the truck as Lily continued driving, uncertainly, towards their new life together.

As the truck disappeared out of Grandma Roberts' sight, she and Lucy slowly turned and made their way back into the house. Mrs Grey was still standing clumsily in the hallway. "Lucy, thank you for being such a brave girl for your little sister," said Mrs Grey uneasily. "That really helped me a lot."

Lucy stared vacantly at Mrs Grey before turning and walking towards the kitchen. "I didn't do it for you," she muttered under her breath, but with just enough volume.

"I'm sorry," mouthed Grandma Roberts at the younger woman, but Mrs Grey shook her head and waved away the apology: *It's absolutely fine, don't worry.*

Mrs Grey was keen to dissolve this uncomfortable moment. "Are you packed up and ready to go to the station now, Mrs Roberts?" she asked.

Grandma Roberts glanced down towards the kitchen. "We had better be making a move now, love," she directed towards Lucy.

Lucy tried to block out their voices. She had one last, very important thing to do. She began to rummage through her mum's cookbooks, looking purposefully for a particular recipe. She picked up book after book and flicked decisively through page after page. She finally found what she was looking for…the recipe for Penny's famous shepherd's pie. The creases and marks on the page revealed just how much it had been used…and loved. With the book tucked tenderly but protectively under her arm, she retraced her steps to the hallway. "I'm ready now, Grandma," she said courageously.

Grandma Roberts glanced down at her brave Lucy. She seemed so much smaller and more fragile than her fourteen years. There was only one, despairing question in Grandma Roberts's mind as she watched this vulnerable child…*why?*

Mrs Grey reached gratefully towards the front door, opened it and stepped out into the welcome air. She couldn't remember being trained for days like this. She took in some much-needed breaths as she and Lucy carried the remaining bags to her car. Grandma Roberts slowly closed the front door. There was an audible, final 'click' as she turned the key to lock the door. "Oh, George, my son. My poor boy. Why did you have to leave? It should have been me first," she whispered sorrowfully. But now was not the time for *her* grief, so she took a deep, steadying breath, looked up and marched towards the awaiting car.

Grandma Roberts opened the door of the passenger seat and climbed in. She turned around to find Lucy gazing out of her window, her expression completely unreadable. Mrs Grey turned the key in the ignition, and pulled the car and her passengers away from the house.

The three unlikely travelling companions were soon at the station and Mrs Grey pulled into the 'drop off' bay, and turned off the ignition. She twisted in her seat to face Lucy. "If there are any problems in the future with anyone or anything," she said kindly, "you have my number. No matter what it is regarding, you can give me a call, anytime. OK?"

Lucy did not respond. Instead, she unclipped her seat belt, picked up her book and briskly exited the car. Grandma Roberts turned to Mrs Grey. She knew now that she didn't need to apologise for Lucy's coldness. The two women were only too well aware of the unthinkable nightmare the girls were living in.

"Thank you for all of your help," she said. "With everything." The moment was almost too huge to bear, so she stepped out of the car. It was all she had the energy to do.

Lucy was already at the boot. She filled her arms with as many bags and cases as she could possibly hold, and began to make her way through to the platform. "Let me take some of those bags, love," offered Grandma Roberts as she followed behind.

"Nope. It's OK, Grandma. I've got them," she said robotically, despite her heavy burden and unsteady steps.

Later that evening, Lucy climbed the stairs of her grandma's house, feeling numb. She had visited many times before, of course, but somehow it seemed as if she had never set foot in this unfamiliar place. She dragged her limp body into what was now her new bedroom, turned on her bedside lamp and slid under the strange duvet. She scanned the room, in a daze, but had no idea what she was looking for. As the fear, grief and sadness flowed cruelly around her veins and brutally settled into her bones, she screwed her eyes tightly shut. She searched the blackness for even the slightest trace of hope, but could find none. The room too was then plunged into darkness as Lucy reached across and turned off the light. The only sound that could now be heard was her faintly singing,

"Ring-a-ring o' roses,
A pocket full of PONIES,
A-tishoo! A-tishoo!
We all fall down!"

***

As Lily's truck pulled through the farm gates, after what seemed like a lifetime, the headlights illuminated all sorts of unfamiliar sights and shapes. Sarah huddled even more deeply into her seat and hugged her knees to her chest. Lily brought the truck to a standstill next to the main house and gratefully switched off the engine. The farmhouse door was suddenly flung open and three boys of varying sizes came running out at top speed. Lily opened her door and climbed out. She breathed a thankful sigh as she stretched out her aching muscles and greeted her sons. "Hi, boys," she said as she kissed each of them on the top of their head. "Are you all ready for bed?"

"Mummy! Where's Sarah?" enquired her eldest. "We want to meet her before we go up."

Lily closed the truck door and lowered her voice. "No, it's time for bed, boys. Let Sarah get settled first and you can all see her in the morning. It has been a very long day for her."

Sarah continued to sit, wide-eyed and motionless in her seat, as she warily watched the three boys scamper back through the door and into the house. But she looked away as she noticed a man now standing just inside the doorway. Her attention was suddenly drawn to the sound of the boot opening and Lily taking out the bags and boxes. The man walked over to the truck, kissed Lily on the cheek and took the cases from her. "How was it?" he enquired carefully.

"Oh, Fergus," she said. "It's all just so heart-breaking." Fergus knew there would be a time to have this conversation with his wife, but it wasn't now. He leaned down to get a better look at Sarah, who was still cowering in the front seat.

He smiled easily as he set off back to the house, and shouted over his shoulder, "You best come in, young lass. I've just made hot chocolate, with extra marshmallows and cream, just for you."

Lily opened Sarah's door and gestured for her to climb out. "Come on, sweetheart," she said gently. "Let's get you settled in." Sarah unhappily took off her seat belt and stepped, exhausted, out into the cool, frosty air. The sky seemed enormous and was filled with a million stars. Lily walked towards the house, but Sarah stopped for a moment and stared up into the sky, anxiously searching the vast expanse for the brightest stars…anxiously searching for her mummy and daddy.

"Come on in, lass, before you catch a chill," said Lily. Sarah walked shyly into what was now her new home. But it was all too much for her to take in and she retreated inside herself even further.

"What would you like to do, love?" asked Lily tentatively. "Would you like to do the evening checks with me, or would you like to see your room and get settled?"

"I want to go to bed," said Sarah quietly but decisively. Lily looked uncertainly at Fergus but he silently handed Sarah her hot chocolate and directed Lily's gaze towards the staircase: *go on.*

Lily picked up a couple of Sarah's bags and led her through the living room and up the stairs. Sarah followed wordlessly behind. Lily paused when she reached the second door on the landing and pushed it open. The door creaked a little on its old hinges. "This is going to be your room, Sarah," she said expectantly. "That's my old teddy, sitting on the bed there. He was mine when I was a little girl." She then pointed towards some shelves. "And there are some story books there for you too. I know it's probably not quite how you want it, so tomorrow we'll go into town and choose some things together, you know, to really make it your room." Lily stood, unsure of what to do or say next.

Sarah pushed past her, placed her hot chocolate on the bedside table and climbed into bed, still in her clothes. She turned purposefully away from Lily and pulled the duvet up high around her face. Lily was lost. "Oh, Penny," she whispered. "I'm so sorry. Please tell me what to do." She waited for a response, but there was none. The terrified little girl before her seemed completely unreachable, so she made the decision to leave her alone with her thoughts. "I am just next door with your Uncle Fergus," she offered before she left. "If you need anything at all, and I mean anything, you come and get me, no matter what time of night it is. I'll leave my door open. OK?" She loitered in the doorway a little longer, just in case, but Sarah didn't move. Lily hesitantly pulled the door almost closed, but left a small gap to let in at least a little bit of light. She paused outside on the landing, but the only sound she could hear was Sarah gently singing:

"Ring-a-ring o' roses,
A pocket full of PONIES,
A-tishoo! A-tishoo!
We all fall down!"

Judgement

Lucy stood mindlessly in front of her calendar. Her pen moved across it, almost on its own, to draw a thick, black 'X' on today's space. It was the start of day six living with her Grandma Roberts. She fastened the pen to the little clip on the side as her eyes scanned the empty squares yet to be crossed off. She let out a long sigh of resignation.

Lucy turned back to face her immaculate room, to make one final check. She walked over to her already perfect bed, but ran her hand across the duvet anyway, to iron out some imaginary creases. She walked towards her bedroom door, took hold of the brass handle, but paused a moment. The house was still and silent. All she could hear was the steady, rhythmic sound of her own breath. With her shoulders squared, she opened the door and stepped out onto the landing. Her descent down the stairs was precise and regimented; she knew exactly how many steps she would have to tread before reaching the bottom. She walked automatically to the kitchen, filled the kettle accurately to the '2-Cup' marker and started to set the table neatly for breakfast.

Grandma Roberts stood silently in the doorway, watching her granddaughter move methodically through the kitchen. She coughed quietly to signal her presence, hoping not to startle Lucy. But the girl jumped like a frightened gazelle who had suddenly realised it was not alone, and dropped the plate she was holding. Time seemed to run in slow-motion as it smashed onto the tiles and filled the kitchen with a sharp, invasive sound.

Lucy let out an alarmed gasp. "Oh! Don't worry, Grandma," she said, frantically. "I'll sort it!" And she immediately scurried to the cupboard to get the dust pan and brush.

Grandma Roberts watched sadly, with deep concern, as Lucy fell to her knees to clear up the broken pieces.

The older lady suddenly clapped her hands together, hoping to divert Lucy's attention away from this meaningless task. "So, what shall we do today, Lucy?" she asked with forced cheeriness.

Lucy continued to sweep up the shards of plate. "Nothing, thank you, Grandma," she said, her voice cold and formal again. "I have to go to the shops, as we need bread and milk. Then I need to hoover the lounge and wash the towels. And the bins are being collected tomorrow so I need to take those out."

Grandma Roberts listened, disheartened, to Lucy's run-down of her chores, just like she had done each day since her arrival. She sat down heavily at her kitchen table, knowing it was pointless even trying to pull Lucy away from this role of 'housekeeper' that she seemed so determined to hide behind.

When Lucy was satisfied that the kitchen was spotless once more, she walked silently into the living room. She seated herself carefully in the armchair, tucked her legs neatly beneath her and picked up her phone from the side-table; a welcome distraction. She turned it on and went immediately to her Facebook page. There was a new 'Friends Request': Molly Richards. Lucy frowned. She couldn't place the name at first, but then disjointed images slowly started to fill her mind; summer holidays at Grandma's, roller-skates, grazed knees, the little girl who lived just two streets away, sleep-overs, sneaky midnight snacks. She started to see that younger girl in the now-teenage face looking back at her from the screen. With her curiosity piqued, Lucy went to Molly's profile page and started to scroll down through her posts.

She was cruelly bombarded with photo after photo of a smiling Molly, with her arms around her smiling parents. Lucy felt a burning rage begin to flow around her body, like poisonous venom. She could feel her fingers gripping the phone tighter and tighter. Her skin began to prickle and her jaw clenched into a hardened, angry line.

A particularly hurtful photo halted Lucy's torturous searching dead in its tracks. It was of Molly and her parents, sitting on a park bench. Molly's dad had his arm draped lovingly around his daughter and she was snuggling into the crook. Her mum was seated beside them, gazing at them and laughing. The bright, autumn colours surrounding them harshly illuminated their already too-sunny smiles. The thin thread that had been holding Lucy together, snapped. "What the…?" she stammered. "Why is she…? How on earth…?" Her fury left little room for the words she was trying so desperately to speak.

"How…could she…? What is she…trying to…? Why is she…sending me a Friends Request? Just…to…rub my face in it?" Lucy's whole body shook. Before she had chance to think, she quickly clicked on the 'Comments' box. Her fingers seemed to take on a life of their own as they rapidly typed angry word after angry word. "OMG! I thought the whole reason somebody sent you a Friends Request was that they actually wanted to be your friend!!! I hope you have loads of fun with your mum and dad! Be careful you don't fall off that bench and break your head! You can totally shove your Friends Request! It is totally DECLINED!" Lucy stabbed at the 'Send' icon and furiously threw the phone back onto the table. Her bitterness continued to grow with every trembling breath she took.

***

"Come on, Molly. Come out and talk to me, sweetheart."

Molly pulled her knees further into her chest and her favourite teddy bear even closer.

"I don't want to talk about it," sniffled Molly sadly. "You saw her comment," she added as the tears rolled unrelentingly down her cheeks.

Ruth, Molly's mum, listened from outside her daughter's bedroom door. She rested her head wearily on the cool wood. *Why now?* she wondered miserably to herself. *This is not what Molly needs.*

Molly's tears were showing no sign of giving up so Ruth slowly opened the door and stepped into her bedroom. She sat down on the end of Molly's bed and waited patiently for her daughter to uncurl herself from the little ball of distress she was currently in. "I can see how upset you are, sweetheart. You must feel really hurt by what Lucy said to you. It's OK to feel upset though. But perhaps, let's see if we can work this out. I know what you went through when Dad and I divorced, love, and how unbelievably lost you felt. And I know that's why you've tried to make contact with Lucy again. How about, when you're ready, we'll try to see this from Lucy's side too, and then work out a way to bring you two back together?"

Molly gently sat up and wiped her eyes. "I just thought we could be there for each other," she said with wide-eyed innocence. "I know it's not even nearly the same but we've both lost our parents, just in different ways." Ruth fidgeted uncomfortably. It never got easier hearing her daughter speak of the heartache she had suffered as a direct result of the divorce. "I know, love," she said warmly. "If there could have been any other way, Dad and I would have done it. I know you won't believe me at all right now, and that's OK, but we honestly believe that our divorce will ultimately make your life better." Molly looked at her, confusion causing her brow to furrow. Ruth continued. "Well, now you have two happy homes, rather than one unhappy house, and a happy mum and a happy dad, rather than two unhappy parents. I truly feel that you'll understand, in time."

Ruth eventually managed to coax a much calmer Molly downstairs with the promise of some milk and homemade flapjack. They sat comfortably together at the kitchen table, and Ruth felt it would be OK now to take their conversation a little further. "Don't forget, love," she began, "Lucy doesn't know anything about mine and Dad's divorce. All she has seen are a few photos on Facebook and assumed that's how we are today." Molly looked thoughtful as she took in her mum's words. "And let's take a moment to think about how Lucy is feeling right now," Ruth continued. "She has just been through the most unimaginable tragedy of losing both her parents, forever. It doesn't even bear thinking about," she added sadly, closing her eyes. "So, let's not make the same mistake and start assuming things about Lucy and her life just because of one Facebook comment. Instead, how about you talk to her and share the truth about what's been going on in your life, and listen to what's been happening in hers? Mrs Roberts has given me Lucy's number," she said as she gently slid a piece of paper towards Molly.

Molly picked up her phone and held it uncertainly in her hand. "Can't I just send her a text, Mum?" she asked, trying to avoid eye-contact with Ruth.

"I'm not sure that would help, love," replied Ruth carefully. "We've just seen how misunderstood a photo and a comment can be, and the upset that that can cause. So, how about you call and actually talk to her? That way, any misunderstanding can be discussed. It's also so much easier to connect with someone when you're speaking to them directly," she offered. Molly took a big, nervous breath, keyed in the numbers and pressed call. She tentatively brought the phone to her ear and waited to hear the sound of her long-missed childhood friend.

Lucy was still sitting in the chair when she suddenly heard the 'Incoming Call' ringtone of her phone. She froze. She watched it as if it was a coiled snake, unsure whether or not any sudden movement would cause it to bite. "Aren't you going to answer that, love?" enquired Grandma Roberts from the kitchen, pulling Lucy out of her trance.

Lucy's movements were slow and calculated but she finally reached out a reluctant hand and pressed 'Accept'.

"Um, hi, Lucy?" said Molly in an almost inaudible whisper. "It's Molly Richards," she added.

"Hey," replied Lucy hesitantly. She had known it would be Molly. But the only sound that followed was the faint static between them on the line. Ruth motioned for Molly to continue and it was she who eventually broke the awkward silence. "I think what you said on Facebook wasn't very nice, Lucy," she said, in what she hoped sounded like a brave voice. "I wanted us to be in touch again so that we could, perhaps, talk to each other and meet up, now that you're so close by. I heard what happened, Lucy," she added quietly. "And, even though it's totally not the same, I've been through something really tough too."

Lucy tightened her grip on the phone and closed her eyes. "Tough!?" she yelled into it. "What the hell have you been through that's tough?! Your life is perfect!" she added, unable to hide the bitterness in her voice.

"Why on earth would you think my life is perfect?" Molly shot back, suddenly angry too.

"Um, duh, have you not seen your Facebook posts?" Lucy asked sarcastically.

Molly paused and then glanced across at her mum for some much needed moral support. Ruth gave her an encouraging nod. "Did you not bother to check when I posted those photos?!" cried Molly. "They were mostly taken two years ago…when my parents were still together! But now they're not and it has been hell! My dad moved out, Mum was crying all the time, they were arguing, I had to miss school, and when I had to stay at my dad's, I had none of my things there. He didn't even have furniture for ages. My family broke too!" she sobbed.

Ruth wrapped her arm around her brave girl's shoulders. She squeezed her with pride, as she had done many times this last two years.

Molly suddenly heard a very small voice down the phone. "I didn't know," whispered Lucy.

"Don't worry," replied Molly with a little more warmth now. "No one knows. I didn't want to be my school's gossip. You're pretty much the only one who does know," she added.

Lucy remained silent as Molly's words filtered through her mind. The anger she felt towards her, just a few moments earlier, started to weaken. But in place of the anger, came shame, like an unwelcome visitor who had barged his way in and settled himself untidily into her favourite chair. Lucy was left trapped in a whirlpool of self-critical thoughts and questions: *Why did I do that? Why am I so stupid? I am such a horrible person. Why the hell would she want to be friends with me now?*

* Sarah *

"Sarah, breakfast's ready!" called Aunt Lily from the bottom of the stairs. Sarah huddled deeper into her bed and pulled the duvet up over her head in protest. She let out a little sigh, closed her eyes and began to whisper to herself.

"I wish I was back home with Mum and Dad," over and over and over. She squeezed her eyes even more tightly shut, hoping somehow that when she opened them again, this room would have vanished.

"That means now, Sarah," Aunt Lily shouted, interrupting Sarah's daydreams.

Sarah reluctantly peeled back her duvet and reached over to open the drawer of her bedside cabinet. She took out her diary and flicked through the pages. Day six. She picked up her pencil just as a warrior might pick up a weapon before battle. The paper tore and the lead snapped as she scratched words crossly onto the page; '*Just about to start another day at this yucky place!*'

In an unwilling act of submission, Sarah quickly pulled on her clothes and made her way downstairs. She was greeted by the usual whirlwind: noisy boys at the kitchen table eating breakfast; excitable dogs running in loops but losing their grip on the tiles; the hay-man loudly slurping tea whilst talking to Uncle Fergus; Aunt Lily busily cooking eggs and bacon on the Aga and speaking rapidly into the phone, yet again; and the rumbling sound of tractors outside. The barrage of too many sights, sounds and smells was still so overwhelming.

A cautious Sarah walked gingerly over to the table and took what was now her seat. Her favourite of the dogs came to sit, optimistically, by her side, just in case a morsel of breakfast should 'accidentally' fall to the floor. Aunt Lily hurriedly brought across a plate of scrambled eggs and bacon, and plonked it distractedly in front of her. "Yes, of course," instructed Aunt Lily into the phone. "Bring that feed at 11 a.m. and I'll put it straight into the store."

Sarah reached nervously across to the toast rack. There was just one slice left.

"That's mine!" shouted Aunt Lily's middle boy, Alec, and he snatched it before Sarah's fingers had even touched it.

"But I haven't had a piece yet," Sarah responded shyly.

"Don't care!" Alec replied as he crudely licked the toast and placed it smugly on his plate.

Sarah stopped. Her face turned an angry shade of red and her body started to shake, like a thunder cloud rolling in, getting ready to unleash its strength. She picked up her plate and slammed it onto the floor. The noise ricocheted around the kitchen as it smashed against the tiles. Time stood still as everyone and everything stopped. All eyes were on this confused and lost little girl as she stormed towards the back door and grabbed her coat and wellies.

Sarah's socks soaked up the wet, farm mud as soon as she stepped outside. She glanced down at the wellies she was still gripping, as if someone else had placed them in her hand without her noticing. She promptly threw them across the yard, as hard as she could, not wanting to touch anything associated with this place! Her rage and frustration carried her little legs towards one of the barns, but she didn't really know where she was going. She didn't really care.

As she entered the gloomy barn, Sarah noticed an old rickety ladder leading to the hay loft. An escape! She ran to it and began to climb, blindly reaching with her hands and feet. As she stepped up onto one of the rungs, it began to break. Sarah almost tumbled but quickly grabbed the next step and scurried to the top. She stood a moment to catch her breath, then sat gratefully amongst the hay with her legs hanging over the edge of the raised loft floor, and her now familiar tears stinging her eyes.

Sarah's attention was suddenly drawn to Mr McGever and his son, Brody, entering the barn. Sarah thought she remembered overhearing a conversation about Mr McGever being some sort of farmer who worked for Aunt Lily and Uncle Fergus. She could hear them talking about a new tractor that was due for delivery at the farm, 'any day now.'

Sarah silently rolled her eyes at Brody bouncing around in excitement. "Can I be the first to have a ride in it, Dad!?" he asked eagerly. Mr McGever nodded and smiled over his shoulder as he exited the barn. No doubt there was some muddy problem that needed attending to.

Brody began to follow his dad but a slight movement in the loft caught his eye. He glanced up and noticed Sarah. "I'll catch up with you, Dad," he called after Mr McGever as he bent down and pretended to tie his boot laces. As soon as his dad was out of earshot, he shout-whispered up to Sarah. "Hey! No one is allowed up there." Sarah didn't move. "The ladder isn't safe, and you'll get into trouble," Brody continued with almost genuine concern. "Quick! Come down before Dad gets back."

"Shut up!" hissed Sarah in response. "No smelly boy is going to tell me what to do! I can do what I want! I'm staying up here so get lost before you get me in trouble," she added rudely. She impulsively lashed out with her foot and kicked at the ladder. It fell to the ground with a loud clatter, narrowly missing Brody.

Sarah shuffled back into the hay-shadows with wide, shocked eyes as Mr McGever raced back into the barn, having been alerted by the commotion. "Brody," he snapped forcefully. "I have told you to stay away from that ladder!" Mr McGever picked it up and placed it carefully back against the edge of the hay loft. "I can't lose you as well," he said as he clutched Brody's shoulders, his words heavy with emotion.

"Mum didn't die from a falling ladder, Dad," Brody answered cheekily but lovingly, teasing his big, soft dad. "It was cancer and it was sooooooo long ago! Besides, she lives in the stars now any way, and I see her every night. And yes, I always tell her about my day, just like you told me to."

Mr McGever took a step back to get a better look at his son. "When did my boy get so grown up?" he asked with proud, shining eyes. "I can't believe you're only eleven."

Mr McGever pulled his son into a long, affectionate hug. "Oh by the way, Brody," he said reflectively. "Whilst we're on that subject…you know we were talking about little Sarah who has just moved in with Lily and Fergus?" Brody nodded and motioned for his dad to continue. "Well, it's obviously been a bit rough for the young lass recently, and she'll be needing a friend," he said encouragingly.

"But she's nothing but trouble," replied Brody, a little more loudly.

"Well, if you see her, be kind to her, eh? I reckon it would be good if we all watched out for her, just while she gets her little head straight," replied Mr McGever.

Brody paused and thought for a moment, aware that Sarah could still hear every word, so he was reluctant to say too much. "We're doing all right though, aren't we, Dad? Me and you?" he asked with unshakable certainty.

"Aye, yes, son. Yes, we are," answered his dad with a warm smile. Mr McGever lovingly ruffled Brody's hair before heading back out to his farm work.

Sarah began to crawl, uncertainly, back out towards the edge of the hay loft. She peered cautiously over the edge at Brody. She couldn't stop thinking about the conversation she had just heard. It was stirring up all sorts of feelings inside her, but she couldn't work out what they were. Unhappiness? Sympathy? Guilt? Relief? She wasn't sure, but didn't think she wanted to find out, so quickly shook the thoughts off before they had chance to settle in. Anger was her loyal sidekick at the moment…and that was just fine with her.

She retraced her steps back down the ladder, with just a little more attention this time. As she reached the bottom rung and turned to leave the barn, she was greeted by a very up-close Brody. He was standing with his hands on his hips, his nose nearly touching hers. This sudden invasion into her now well-protected personal space caused Sarah to lose her footing. She stumbled clumsily and fell back, tripping over the foot of the ladder, straight into some mud. Brody sniggered as he stood over her. "So," he said sarcastically. "You decided to finally do as you're told?"

Sarah hastily got to her feet and brushed the clumps of mud from her trousers. "No," she replied defensively. "I, err...just have...um, just have...to go somewhere," she stuttered as she pushed past him.

"Well, I could come with you," suggested Brody. Sarah quickened her pace and began to walk across the yard, eyes down, hands in pockets. Brody followed, not quite willing to give up his pursuit just yet. "Well, I know all the good hiding places around here," he directed at her small, hunched shoulders.

"Yeah, so what?" Sarah shot back.

"Well, duh," said Brody. "I thought you'd want more places to hide. So, you know, why don't we be friends, or something. I could show you?" Brody continued.

But Sarah stormed straight through the gate and into the field. She left Brody standing in the yard with just a few harsh, parting words. "I don't want you to come with me!" she yelled over her shoulder. "Why the heck would I want to be friends with you?"

Courage

Lucy stood, once again, in front of her calendar. She was just about to mark the current space with a now familiar, black 'X', but realised that today was different. Written in small, green letters were the words '*Tea with Molly*'. A tentative, tiny smile crept across her face; she didn't resist it. And she didn't double-check her tidy room and she didn't pause at the door and she didn't robotically count her descent down the stairs. Today, she almost skipped. She made her way into the kitchen to start her usual morning routine, but instead of turning just the kettle on, she turned on the radio too. As a familiar, happy tune filled the room, Lucy started to hum quietly.

Grandma Roberts tiptoed across the hallway, intrigued by the unfamiliar yet cheery sound emanating from the kitchen. It was music to her ears! She took her seat at the table and Lucy kindly placed her grandma's tea and toast in front of her – a well-practised move on both their parts now. Grandma Roberts silently studied her granddaughter, as a person might study a snowdrop trying to break through the frozen, winter soil. She wanted so desperately to acknowledge this long-awaited glimpse of a change in Lucy's behaviour, but knew that any intervention could disrupt this oh-so delicate process.

A comfortable silence settled between Lucy and her grandma, and the radio continued to fill the kitchen with its happy beat. But despite Lucy's building excitement, she could no longer ignore the nervous knot beginning to tighten in her tummy. She had yet to ask Grandma Roberts about tea with Molly. It was now or never. Why was she so nervous?! Why was this so hard? It was such a simple request…wasn't it? She picked up her mug of tea and swirled the liquid around and around, stalling for time, perhaps hoping to see the words drift helpfully from her cup. She watched the tea-whirlpool gathering speed as she gathered her courage. *Just do it.*

"Grandma?" Lucy finally squeaked, nervously.

Grandma Roberts paused and looked curiously across the table at Lucy. "Yes, love," she replied tentatively. She sensed that Lucy was about to begin what was an incredibly difficult conversation for her, and she did not want to be the reason that Lucy changed her mind. She waited patiently for her brave granddaughter to continue.

"Well," began Lucy hesitantly. "If it's OK with you, and it's totally OK if it isn't. I mean, I don't have to…you can totally say no, and it's fine, it really is…but I would get everything sorted, and you wouldn't have to worry about anything…but you really can say no," she continued breathlessly.

"What is it, love?" interrupted Grandma Roberts gently.

"Well, Molly has invited me round for tea," Lucy spluttered out, as if saying it quickly might somehow make it seem less of a big deal.

Lucy's gaze dropped. Silence followed. A look of joyful shock slowly started to spread across Grandma Robert's face, but she quickly tried to hide it behind her mug of tea. Could this be the day that she had been so patiently waiting for? The day that things were beginning to change? She took a deep, relaxing breath – now was not the time to release her delight and the gleeful smirk trying to take form. "Yes, that's absolutely fine, love," she replied, trying to sound calm and casual. She picked up some of yesterday's unopened post and faked distraction. "I need to go and see Rita anyway to… OUCH!"

Lucy looked up, startled. She gasped as she saw what she thought was a grimace of pain cross her grandma's face, and blood on her hand.

"Grandma?!" Lucy enquired with frightened concern.

"It's absolutely nothing, love," Grandma Roberts said chirpily as she waved away Lucy's alarm. "I just caught my finger on a staple. It looks much worse than it is."

Lucy had barely even begun to slow her breathing in the time it took her grandma to get back to the table: finger washed, Band-Aid applied, cup of tea back in hand.

"Oh, Grandma! Don't worry!" Lucy said, with a trace of panic in her voice. "I'll just tell Molly that I can come round another day. It's OK," said Lucy.

Grandma Roberts paused. She had to think very carefully about how she was going to phrase her next sentence. The significance of Lucy's invitation to Molly's was not lost on her, but selfishly, she also wanted an evening with her own friend, to talk openly about the pain of losing her son, George. "Honestly, Lucy," she began, but with a little more insistence now, "I think I'll survive," she said with a wink as she held up her finger. "And besides, I'd really like to see Rita, and I think you'll enjoy not having to listen to me babble on about how we didn't have mobile phones back in my day," she added, and then swiftly left the kitchen with nothing but a chuckle and, if you looked really closely, a twinkle in her eye.

Any thought Lucy may have had about arguing the point with her grandma was interrupted by the 'incoming text' tone on her phone. It was Molly. "*Hey! Still OK for 2nite? So excited! Mum said we can have fish n chips. Got so much 2 tell you, even tho I only spoke to you yesterday...and the day before! Haha! Xx*". Lucy paused – a small ball of fear started to bounce recklessly inside her heart, and for just a split-second she contemplated telling Molly that she couldn't make it. But she knew deep down that this was not the truth – that this was not her truth. So she typed her reply. "*Yes! Definitely! 5pm still OK? Can't wait!*" And she realised that a tiny part of her couldn't.

The hours passed quickly as Lucy happily carried out her usual chores. Grandma Roberts watched her buzz around the house, not wanting to miss a single moment. A short time later, they walked companionably together to Rita's house, where Lucy waved goodbye to her grandma. As Grandma Roberts watched her walk away, she noticed a lightness to Lucy's step that she hadn't seen for a very long time, and that a pretty skirt and bright top had replaced her all too familiar faded jeans and black t-shirt. Before knocking on her friend's door, Grandma Roberts smiled, looked up to the sky and whispered, '*Thank you.*'

But it wasn't long before the lightness in Lucy's step grew a little heavier. As she continued her journey to the house with the blue door that she had known so well as a child, the fear inside her began to rise, like a climbing weed-plant looking for holds to cling to. She flinched at the sound of a dog barking and momentarily lost her footing, almost slipping into the road. The driver in a passing car beeped their horn loudly, breaking what was left of Lucy's nerve – she felt dizzy and confused, as if she was suddenly swimming through this now-alien, watery world. *Breathe*, she said to herself. *All you have to do right now is just breathe.*

***

Molly had been waiting at the lounge window since about 4:00 p.m.! As the minute hands tick-tocked their steady countdown to her friend's arrival, her fidgeting grew worse, and she pressed her nose even harder against the window that looked out onto the street. If excitement alone was enough to make Lucy appear, she would have been here hours ago! Ruth chuckled at this endearing scene. And then, Lucy was finally in sight! Molly sprang out of her front door and waved her arms frantically in Lucy's direction.

Lucy caught sight of her bouncy friend, and chose, in that moment, to swallow her doubts and continue to put one foot in front of the other. Before she had even reached the bottom of the path, Molly was already chattering away at great speed. "Come in, Lucy," she exclaimed excitedly. "Come in! I have everything set up for us in the living room! And Mum's letting us have our fish and chips in front of a movie! But I couldn't decide which one!"

Ruth appeared behind her daughter. "Give Lucy chance to get through the door, love!" she said with a smile, before turning to Lucy. "Hi, sweetheart. Come on in," she said warmly. "Now, how about you girls go and choose your film and I'll get your dinner?"

Molly dragged Lucy into the living room and across to her DVD collection. "You can totally choose," she said kindly to her friend. "But, I did put my five favourites in this pile here, just in case you like one of them," she added with a grin.

Lucy glanced at the titles and couldn't help but smile a shy smile as she realised that they were all her favourites too. "I think this one?" enquired Lucy cautiously, hoping so much that it was a choice her friend would be happy with.

Molly took the DVD from her and gave a little jump in the air. "Yes!" she exclaimed. "I wanted you to pick that one! I love that bit when they fall in love and go walking in the rain and have their first kiss! Just like Mum and her new boyfriend, Luke! Mum and Luke, sitting in a tree, K-I-S-S-I-N-G!" Molly sang mischievously, just as Ruth re-entered the room.

"Oi, cheeky little lady!" Ruth said affectionately. Molly giggled, skipped across the room to put on the DVD and then plonked herself contentedly into her over-sized beanbag. Lucy stood nervously in the middle of the room, trying to decide where to sit, trying to find her place. Ruth could sense Lucy's uneasiness and quickly suggested she take the sofa next to Molly. Lucy quietly obeyed and hesitantly made her way across the living room. She perched neatly but uncomfortably on the edge of the seat – a sprinter on the starting blocks, ready to flee at the sound of the pistol.

As Ruth heard the movie come to an end and Molly begin an excited run-down of every single scene, she made her way back into the living room. "Would you girls like some ice cream?"

"Woohoo! Yes please, Mum," answered Molly enthusiastically as she wiggled deeper into her beanbag.

Ruth turned hopefully to Lucy: *And you*?

"No, thank you," Lucy replied quietly as she readjusted her skirt and glanced anxiously at her watch.

"Molly?" said Ruth. "Be a love and go and fetch three bowls of ice cream from the kitchen please."

Ruth waited for Molly to leave the room before sitting carefully next to Lucy on the sofa. Just a quick glimpse of this poor, lost girl immediately transported Ruth back to the moment she and Molly's dad had to break the news to her about the divorce. It was all so painfully familiar and her heart broke for them both.

Ruth leaned a little towards Lucy. "How's your grandma, love?" she began, hoping to put her at ease, just a little. "Please do tell her I said hello and that I'll pop in for a cup of tea again soon."

Lucy continued to stare at her skirt and gave a tiny nod.

"And how are you, sweetheart?" Ruth continued sympathetically. "Are you settling in OK there?"

Lucy paused a moment and finally looked at Ruth. There was so much she wanted to say but all she managed was a robotic, *"Fine, thanks."*

Ruth placed her hand warmly on Lucy's arm. "How's it really going, love?" she urged gently.

There was something in Ruth's voice – Lucy's carefully constructed defence started to wobble on its foundations and her tear ducts began to fill. "I'm OK, I guess, and getting used to living with Grandma Roberts," she added softly. "But I just still really miss them," she said with a small sob.

"Of course you do, love," replied Ruth tenderly. "How on earth could you not? It's absolutely fine to still miss them, my darling," she added reassuringly. "But, it's also fine to have a break once in a while and watch movies and eat ice cream and watch Molly bounce around and get lost in your daydreams."

Ruth gently placed her hand on Lucy's hair before heading to the kitchen, to help Molly. Lucy sat very still for a moment as she digested Ruth's words. She shuffled back, just slightly, into the sofa and allowed her mind to wander back to the last day she and Sarah had played together in the attic, with their beloved box. She thought that was probably the last time she had been truly happy. She slowly closed her eyes and wished with all her might that she could have that feeling again…even for just one day.

* Sarah *

Aunt Lily's now-familiar breakfast announcement drifted up the stairs and into Sarah's bedroom, pulling her out of sleep. "Come on, Sarah. It's getting cold!" Aunt Lily added loudly.

Sarah leaned over to retrieve her diary from the drawer in her bedside cabinet – an almost habitual move now. She opened it up and started to write her usual sentence; '*Another day in this…*' but she stopped before finishing it. She looked out of the window and a small thought began to push sleep aside and take shape in her head. And then she remembered that it was today they were arriving! A tiny smile started to tug at the corner of her

48

mouth as she disentangled herself from her duvet and jumped out of bed.

Sarah somehow managed to coordinate pulling on her clothes *and* pounding down the stairs, miraculously, without causing damage to herself or surrounding objects. It couldn't exactly be described as a smooth move, but she did manage to end up in her seat after some impressive sock-skidding across the kitchen tiles. She reached impatiently for her knife and fork and started shovelling eggs and bacon into her mouth.

Aunt Lily made her way across to the table too and sat down opposite Sarah. "So, Sarah," she said. "Are you looking forward to today?"

Sarah began to nod and speak rapidly at the same time. Lily wasn't sure whether to be disgusted or delighted as she watched pieces of egg fly from Sarah's mouth.

"Yeah!" answered Sarah enthusiastically. "I can't wait for them to get here! Can I still help?" she asked, unable to stop wiggling in her seat.

"Absolutely," confirmed Aunt Lily. "We need all the hands and help we can get. Those sheep are a lot quicker than they look! Uncle Fergus will be back from the market with them soon," Aunt Lily explained just as her and Sarah heard the familiar sound of Mr McGever's truck pulling into the yard.

A resigned '*OK then*' nod and small smile from Lily told Sarah that she was now permitted to leave the table. She jumped out of her seat and darted towards the front door. Patience clearly wasn't on her agenda today!

"Hang on a minute, young lady," instructed Aunt Lily with mock sternness. "Don't you think you're forgetting something?" she asked as she raised her eyebrows at Sarah's abandoned plate. Lily smirked as she watched Sarah retrace her steps, pick up her plate and almost throw it into the dishwasher. She could be picked for the Olympic discus team with a move like that!

"Now can I go?!" asked Sarah impatiently, hopping from one foot to the other. Aunt Lily tutted and rolled her eyes good-naturedly at Sarah's eagerness.

Sarah pulled on her now-loved spotty wellies and coat, before heading out to Mr McGever. The dogs were hot on her heels, unsure of what there was to be excited about but not wanting to miss whatever it might be.

"Morning, young lass," said Mr McGever to the little tornado spinning out of the house.

"Are they on their way? Are they on their way?" asked Sarah, with bright, hopeful eyes. Mr McGever smiled as he started walking towards the sheep shed.

"Aye, they are, lass. They are."

"Can I still help?" Sarah asked excitedly as she tripped after Mr McGever. But he continued to walk silently into the barn – there was important work to be done. The yard was suddenly filled with the unmistakable sound of Uncle Fergus's truck and rattling trailer as it approached the farm.

"Grab that gate for us, lass," directed Mr McGever as he watched Fergus expertly reverse up to the shed. Sarah obediently grabbed the heavy gate. After a great deal of heaving and pulling and tugging, it unexpectedly swung open, and knocked Sarah clean off her feet and flat onto her bottom.

Mr McGever let out a loud chuckle as Sarah scrabbled around in the straw, trying to regain her footing. At the sight of Mr McGever's laughing face, a small ping-pong ball of anger began to jump around in Sarah's tummy, but she stopped it and chose to giggle along at the silliness instead.

Uncle Fergus turned the engine off, stepped out of his truck and made his way to the back of the trailer – his boots made satisfying squelchy noises in the mud. He caught sight of Sarah and Mr McGever still mid-chuckle. "What's so funny?" he asked in amusement as he deftly unclipped the back of the trailer. But before Sarah had chance to respond, the thunder of tiny hooves started to clatter nervously down the ramp.

"Stand back, lass!" roared Mr McGever over the noise. "You don't want to go flying again!"

Sarah swiftly hopped up onto the highest of the gate rungs. She gripped onto the bars tightly with both hands and held her breath as her muscles started to pulse. She gazed from her look-out haven, in awe, at the sea of white wool rolling down the ramp and into the main pen.

As Mr McGever and Uncle Fergus effortlessly drove the last anxious sheep into the pen, Sarah jumped down off the gate, into the bouncy straw, and ran to stand by Uncle Fergus's side. She peeked through the gate-rungs at the woolly sight before her. Uncle Fergus looked in amusement to see Sarah so captivated.

He reached down and patted her lovingly on the back. "I didn't know you had a smile in there," he said to her warmly, before walking away and climbing back into his truck. A farmer's work was never done.

"It's a good flock, Lily," said Mr McGever admiringly as Aunt Lily joined them at the gate.

"So, what's next?" asked Sarah with eager anticipation.

"Sorting is what's next," answered Mr McGever. "We need to divide these sheep into two flocks."

"OK!" shouted Sarah, despite not quite understanding what that meant. "What should I do?" she asked.

Mr McGever lifted up his hat and ruffled his hair. "Well, if you want to go to the other side of the pen and open and close that gate for us to let half the sheep through, I reckon that'll do just fine," he said as he opened the main gate and stepped through into the sea of jumpy sheep.

Mr McGever barely had chance to finish his instruction before Sarah raced round to the other end of the barn and took a firm hold of the second gate. "Ready!" she shouted.

"OK, open the gate now, lass," directed Mr McGever as Lily stepped into the pen to help him guide the first sheep through. "Well done, lass," he said to Sarah as he saw the sheep safely locked in its new pen.

"And again, Sarah!" directed Aunt Lily, threading another ewe through and into the second enclosure.

Sarah became so engrossed in the exciting spectacle before her, and her task of opening and closing the gate, that she didn't notice a particularly mischievous sheep creep up behind her. It began to nuzzle curiously at the back of her knees. Sarah spun around, startled by this suddenly very close animal. The sheep didn't appear to have satisfied its curiosity yet and began to nudge a little harder. Sarah tried desperately to shoo it away *and* keep her balance *and* hold onto the gate, all at the same time, but lost this impossible battle. She stumbled and let go of the gate, then watched with wide, frightened eyes as it flung wide open on its hinges and banged loudly against the metal fence. The metallic noise echoed around the barn, alarming the sheep. There was nothing anybody could do except watch as the frightened animals ran between the two pens and mixed themselves, once again, into one big flock.

Sarah scrabbled to the side of the barn and pinned herself against the wall. She squeezed her eyes tightly shut as her heart began to beat too rapidly and her little lungs gasped for breath. Fear rolled around her body, like huge, dark ocean waves. As she became paralysed with terror, she felt a strong arm scoop her up off the ground. It was Mr McGever.

Sarah nestled her head deep into the crook of his neck. The dam broke and she burst into floods of tears. "I am…so…sorry…" she stuttered through deep, gasping sobs. "I…didn't…mean…to."

Mr McGever soothed the poor, terrified girl in his arms as he gently rocked her from side to side and whispered, *'Everything is going to be all right.'*

Alerted by the commotion, Fergus then re-entered the barn. "Is everything all right?" he asked. "I heard such a noise."

Lily spun around and huffed. "No! Sarah's only just gone and mixed all the sheep up," she said in annoyance. "Now we'll have to start all over again," she added unsympathetically. She glanced down sulkily at her watch. "I don't have time for this," she said harshly. "I need to be gone in half an hour."

Mr McGever cleared his throat to draw both Fergus's and Lily's attention to the panicky girl in his arms, and her tear-stained cheeks. He raised his eyebrows and glared at them: *Don't you dare say another word.*

Lily and Fergus stopped and looked at each other – a shadow of shame started to darken their faces. They quietly made their way into the pen and began to divide the sheep once again, in silence. Mr McGever carried Sarah tenderly out to his truck and placed her down on the tailgate. He waited patiently for the sniffles to subside: *Take your time, lass.* When he felt the time was right, he took out his handkerchief and wiped Sarah's tears. "Today was not your fault, lass," he said reassuringly. "We seem to have a comedian sheep amongst our flock," he added with a smile. "It could have happened to any of us. Maybe that mischievous sheep was looking for a mischievous friend," he chuckled. "Look, lass. You've been through a lot! Don't be too hard on yourself about today. Mistakes happen to everyone. It's what you do after them that counts."

Sarah stopped for a moment and let Mr McGever's words unravel themselves and then take shape again. She began to swing her legs – perhaps stalling for time, or maybe waiting for time to somehow go backwards. She finally looked up at Mr McGever. "I made a mistake," she said in the tiniest whisper.

Mr McGever remained silent but motioned for her to continue.

"I did something horrible when me and Lucy left home," she added hastily. "I took something that was ours! I should have shared it with Lucy! I made a mistake, Mr McGever! How do I fix it?"

Mr McGever felt the sad weight of this little girl's guilt, and moved across to perch just a tiny bit closer to her on the tailgate. This small, sympathetic move urged Sarah on with her confession.

"Well, we had this box. It was our 'What-I-Want-To-Be-When-I-Grow-Up' box, and I just took it, and I was really mean, and now Lucy doesn't have a box, or her dolls!" she sobbed.

Mr McGever lifted his hat and ruffled his hair. "Well, lass," he said reflectively. "It seems to me that we need to find another box, so you and Lucy can have one each." With this, he hopped off the tailgate and walked back towards the barn, deep in thought.

Sarah sniffed and wiped her tears with her sleeve. She allowed her mind to wander back to the last day she and Lucy had played together in the attic, with their cherished box. That was a time she had been really happy. She slowly swung her legs and wished with all her might that she could have that feeling again…even for just one day.

Opportunities

* Lucy *

Lucy's eyes sprung open as a handsome, chirpy blackbird landed on a branch just outside her bedroom window. It sang its note-perfect announcement of a new day as Lucy bounded out of bed and whistled along with the bird. The melody seemed to release her from her shyness, and her dreams started to run like wild horses freed from a corral.

She stood, as usual, in front of her calendar, and wondered how long it had been since she had marked the day with a thick, black 'X'. As her gaze absorbed the array of colourful writing and bright heart stickers now in their place, she realised that she had stopped counting. With one final whistle and a quick nod in the blackbird's direction, she disappeared down the stairs.

Lucy screeched to an impressive halt at the bottom of the stairs as she saw the silhouette of a man through the glass of the front door. The silhouette knocked and Grandma Roberts appeared in the hallway, alerted by the sound. "Don't just stand there, love. It's Carl, the postman," she directed at her open-mouthed granddaughter. "And the door won't open itself," she added cheekily. Lucy laughed at herself and shook off her initial shock. She strode confidently to the front door and greeted Carl with a cheery, *"Good morning."*

"Good morning yourself, Miss Lucy," replied Carl with his unmistakable, sunny smile. "I've got something for you today," he said happily as he handed Lucy a large cardboard box.

"For me?" responded Lucy with a puzzled look. "But it's not my birthday."

"Well," said Carl with a wink, before turning around and heading back to his van. "It must just be your lucky day."

Lucy staggered under the weight of the box as she made her way to the kitchen, her excitement growing with each step. She plonked it down on the table with a delightful thud. With shuffling feet and enthusiastic fingers, she ripped it open and peered inside. Lucy let out a large gasp and her hands flew to her mouth.

"What is it, love?" asked Grandma Roberts, unable to contain her own curiosity any longer.

"I don't believe it, Grandma," Lucy exclaimed breathlessly, hardly daring to consider what she thought it was.

She leaned over to get a better look and could barely contain her delight at the sight of a box with '*Lucy*' and '*Sarah*' engraved on the top. There was an envelope with just her name written on it and she recognised the spider-handwriting immediately. "It's from Sarah!" she declared with tears in her eyes. She gazed up at her grandma with a look of pure happiness.

"Well, get it out," instructed Grandma Roberts with an impatient smile.

Lucy carefully lifted up the envelope first. She turned it over and over in her hands as if she was holding something rare and truly wondrous – a precious treasure unearthed from the depths of a cave, after years in darkness. She finally opened it up and slid out a single, folded piece of paper.

To Lucy
Hi. Hope you like your new box! I made it myself! Sorry for taking our box with me. ☹
Love you
Sarah
Xxx

Lucy could not suppress her excitement any longer and promptly turned what was left of the table surface into a sea of shredded newspaper and bubble wrap! She finally set her new, almost identical 'What-I-Want-To-Be-When-I-Grow-Up' box free from its cardboard container. *Is it possible...?* she thought to herself. *Could Sarah really have...?* She took a deep breath, slowly lifted the lid and peeked inside. She saw...a glimmer of white...part of an oh-so familiar book cover...a flash of pink...

Lucy flung the lid back all the way and began to bounce around the kitchen. It was all there! The tiny white, leather purse which had held her mum's wedding ring, her book of Cinderella…and her dolls!

It was quite some time before Lucy's delight subsided enough for her to catch her breath. She was overcome with such emotion, and Grandma Roberts was overcome with such relief.

"I have got to go and show Molly and Ruth," Lucy suddenly declared with renewed excitement.

As Grandma Roberts watched her granddaughter's face glow with life, she did not need to think of what her response should be this time. "Of course, love! Go, go, go," she encouraged without hesitation, and almost knocked Lucy off balance as she, herself, pushed the box into her arms.

***

'Ding dong ding dong ding dong ding dong!' rang Ruth's doorbell frantically. Ruth hurried to open the door, slightly worried about who might need her in such a desperate way. She pulled it wide and was immediately greeted by the sight of a very smiley Lucy, holding a very large box. "What have you got there, Lucy?" asked Ruth with open interest as she stepped aside to let her in. It seemed this box was going to become the talking point of the day.

"You'll never guess!" answered Lucy breathlessly.

"Well, why don't you come and join us," Ruth offered kindly. "Molly and I were just about to tuck into a picnic in the back garden." Ruth motioned for Lucy to head straight through.

"Hi, Luce!" Molly chimed as she saw her friend stepping out into the sunshine and heading over to sit with her on a large blanket.

"Oh my goodness!" Lucy squealed. "You'll never guess in a million years what Sarah has done for me," she added eagerly.

"Ooooo! What? What?" asked Molly inquisitively, already drawn into the excitement.

"It's the box I was telling you about!" declared Lucy with dancing eyes and a wide grin. "You know?" she continued, "the What-I-Want-To-Be-When-I-Grow-Up box," said Lucy with bursting pride, as she opened the lid to show her friend.

"Oh!" replied Molly. "That box you never shut up about!" she added cheekily, as she nudged Lucy playfully with her shoulder.

"Well, it's absolutely wonderful to see you with such a huge smile on that beautiful face, Lucy," said Ruth knowingly.

Lucy looked up into Ruth's eyes. "You have no idea how much me and Sarah used to play with our box!" Lucy said. "We spent hours and hours with it. I used to play with my dolls and dress them up in my designs for their wedding day!"

"Aren't you a bit old to play with dolls?" interjected Molly with an affectionate shove.

"Don't you still have your teddy bears?" Lucy shot back in jest. They both giggled.

"Girls, if it helps you to dream, I'd say it doesn't matter what you play with," mused Ruth wisely.

Ruth shuffled into a more comfortable position on the blanket. "Let me tell you a story," she directed at Lucy and Molly. "It seems to me that this box is more than just a box. It seems to me that it's a piece of you," she added.

Lucy nodded in earnest agreement, so Ruth continued.

"Have you ever heard a story about the path to a dream? About the stepping stones to take and the cracks to avoid? About how, on that journey, you discover and become who you want to be?"

Lucy and Molly both tilted their heads and looked at Ruth quizzically.

"Hmm, OK, then. How about putting it this way," Ruth continued. "Imagine you are sat on a leaf but that leaf is actually a little boat. You are travelling on a river in your little boat, but the river is your life. Sometimes the river will flow calmly and smoothly, and sometimes there will be choppy rapids. Sometimes you will get caught in a dizzy whirlpool and sometimes trapped behind a rock." The girls were both deep in their own thoughts as they absorbed Ruth's words.

"The key is not to fight whatever is happening to your little boat, but to trust that the difficult parts won't last for ever and that there will be good parts on their way. Lucy, sweetheart, you were just caught in the most terrible whirlpool when you lost your mum and dad. But, your big smile today shows me that your little boat is slowly coming out of that whirlpool and into much calmer waters." Lucy's face filled with so many emotions.

"It doesn't mean that what happened to your mum and dad isn't the most awful thing in the world," added Ruth sympathetically. "That will always be with you. But, the other parts of your life, like your friends, your dreams, your new family, your hobby of clothes design, and starting school soon, will all help you through the sadness. You will have other things to look forward to, plans to make, dreams to turn into reality…and it's all of that, as a whole, that makes you who you are."

* Sarah *

Sarah yawned and stretched as she woke to the gentle rustling of branches outside her bedroom window. She rubbed her sleepy eyes and pushed herself up onto her elbows to better discover the cause of the noise. It was her robin, staring back at her.

"Good morning, Mrs Robin," Sarah sang as she climbed out of bed and began to get dressed. "Did you know that today is going to be a good day? For me and for you too, Mrs Robin," she added. "I made my wish last night when I saw a shooting star, so maybe today is the day it will come true! I'll leave your bird seed where I normally do, OK, Mrs Robin?" she said reassuringly as she pulled out her diary and began to write.

But Sarah's attention was suddenly captured by a familiar voice downstairs. It was Mr McGever! She rushed out of her bedroom, bounded down the stairs and into the kitchen, and promptly fell over one of the dogs. A typical Sarah entrance.

"Steady on there, lass," Mr McGever chuckled. Sarah just about managed to untangle her giggling self from the dog, who thought this was all great fun too, and got to her feet. "What's the rush?" Mr McGever asked.

"Lucy got the box! Lucy got the box!" Sarah cried in delight. "She called me last night to tell me! I mended my mistake, Mr McGever," she added gleefully as she hopped from one foot to the other.

"Well done, lass!" answered Mr McGever with loving admiration, and he bent to affectionately ruffle Sarah's hair.

"Ah, now that I've got you here, lass," continued Mr McGever, "Brody's been bugging me to ask if you'd like to come round for your tea again tonight. I've just checked with your Aunt Lily, and she's given the go-ahead."

This seemingly simple question sparked much squealing from Sarah, which in turn, sparked much jumping from the dog. "Oooooo, yes please, Mr McGever!" answered Sarah with undisguised excitement.

"Only if you get all your jobs done, mind," said Mr McGever with mock-seriousness and a sparkle in his eyes.

"I will! I will! I promise!" shouted Sarah as she raced to the door, pulled on her now well-worn wellies, and disappeared outside, her four-legged friend a willing runner in this race.

Sarah galloped across the yard towards the chicken coop, eager to begin her daily chores. A large bucket banged against her legs with each excited step. "Hello there, chickens," she said tenderly. "Did you sleep well last night? How many eggs have you got for me today?" she enquired as she lifted the lid of the roosting box. She carefully reached inside and delicately placed each of her finds into the bucket. Sarah paused as she lifted up an unusually large egg. "Wow!" she declared approvingly. "This is huge! This must be a double-yolker," she added knowingly.

She retraced her steps back to the kitchen, making sure she splashed in every single muddy puddle she met along the way. She careered through the door at Sarah-speed, only just screeching to a stop before she collided with Mr McGever.

"We need to fit some brakes to those wellies," he said with a smile. "Meet me at my truck at 5:00 p.m., lass," he instructed, before heading off to see to his daily chores.

Sarah skipped across to the Aga, where Aunt Lily was standing. "Look at the size of this egg," she declared as she held her prized discovery proudly in front of her.

"Oooo," gushed Lily. "We could make one of your mum's famous lemon drizzle cakes with that! Shall we do that today? You could perhaps then take it with you to Mr McGever's tonight?" she suggested kindly.

"Woohoo! Yes please!" answered Sarah, still unable to keep still. But her face suddenly dropped. "How can we though, Aunt Lily?" she asked, disheartened. "We don't have Mum's recipe."

"Well," answered Lily with a crafty grin. "Maybe this will help us," she said, as she gently took a piece of paper from one of the kitchen drawers. It was a recipe for Lemon Drizzle Cake, written in Penny's unmistakable handwriting. Sarah beamed.

It was finally 5 o'clock. Sarah picked up the still-warm cake tin and ran outside to Mr McGever's waiting truck. Mr McGever breathed in the mouth-watering aromas as Sarah climbed in and filled the truck with lemony goodness. As the truck weaved and rattled its way down the now-familiar country roads, Sarah wound down her window and leaned her head right outside. She craned her neck to look up into the vast array of twinkling stars.

"Brrrrr!" shuddered Mr McGever. "Goodness, lass! We don't want to turn into ice cubes! What are you looking for?" he enquired with a shiver.

"Another shooting star," answered Sarah, matter-of-factly. "You know," she added, "to make a wish."

Mr McGever started to chuckle. "It's not wishes you want to make," he said decisively. "It's dreams! Now, they're the ones that come true!"

Sarah heaved herself back into the truck at these words and wound her window back up, much to Mr McGever's relief.

Sarah turned to face him. "I don't get it, Mr McG," she said with comfortable familiarity.

"Well, wishing for something is actually a bit lazy because all you do is say the words, and then just expect the wish to appear, like magic," he added thoughtfully. "But when you dream, you create a plan, a sort of list of things that need to be done to get you there." Mr McGever was on a roll now. "With dreams, you actually need to get off your bottom and do something about it!" He finished his speech with a wink and a definitive slap of the steering wheel.

Mr McGever finally bounced the truck into his yard and stopped it, just in front of the farmhouse. "Don't you be forgetting that cake," he directed at Sarah as he climbed out. "That'll do just nicely for desert." The friendly pair made their way together into the warmth of the house.

They hadn't even taken their boots off when Brody zoomed into the kitchen. "Hi, Sarah!" he shouted happily. "Come through, quick! I've made a really cool den for us in the living room," he said, tugging impatiently at Sarah's arm. She frantically shook her legs to free her feet from her wellies. They bounced off in different directions and landed, haphazardly, on the floor. She managed a small, not very sincere, apologetic shrug before running after Brody into the living room.

"Your dad's just told me one of his stories," Sarah said playfully as she burrowed under the den-blankets.

"Oh no!" groaned Brody as he rolled his eyes in pretend despair. "Which one this time?" he asked.

"Something about wishes, dreams and bottoms," answered Sarah with a cheeky giggle.

"Oh yeah, *that* one," said Brody, shaking his head and smiling.

Little did they know, but Mr McGever was standing in the living room doorway, listening with delight to the comic double-act. "You two are acting more and more like brother and sister every single day," he said with a quiet, satisfied nod.

The mischievous duo clambered out from under the blankets. Sarah suddenly looked at Brody. "Hey, you'll never guess what!" she said. "Lucy got the box I sent!"

Brody answered coolly with a thumbs up.

"So, what do you want to be when you grow up, Brody?" she enquired curiously.

Brody's expression changed to one of deep thought, for once! "I want to be a farmer, just like my dad. And I'm doing something every day to get me there. So, like tomorrow, I'm going out on the quad to learn how to fix some fencing," he confirmed with pride.

Mr McGever stepped forward and motioned for Sarah to come and stand by him at a large mirror hanging on the wall. "Now, young lass," he said wisely as he pointed at Sarah's reflection. "See that girl?" he asked. Sarah nodded, unsure of where this was heading. "Well, that girl you see is the girl you are now, and the girl you're going to become. And the words that come out of your mouth are going to help get you the life you want."

Sarah continued to stare blankly at Mr McGever. "OK, repeat after me," he instructed. "*I, Sarah, am a country girl. I love animals and I am really good at taking care of them and I'd really like my life to be filled with as many animals as possible!*"

"Ooooo! I get it," Sarah said, nodding with enthusiasm. She pulled some straw out of her hair and looked down at the mud on her trousers. "That's easy though," she said confidently as she looked up at Mr McGever.

"You're right. Some bits are easy," he confirmed. "But don't be fooled, young lass. You do still need to actively do something every day to become the person you want to be. Carry on looking after Aunt Lily's animals as well as you have been, and I'd say that's a pretty big step towards at least one of your dreams coming true."

Sarah was now very much enjoying this 'game'. "Which one?" she asked eagerly.

"The one about wanting your life to be filled with your own animals one day."

Sarah's smile began to widen, but Mr McGever wasn't quite finished.

"But don't you forget, lass, if you just sit in your room, doing nothing, then that dream would probably never come true. Because, that there is just wishful thinking," he added with a wizardry wink.

Changes

Lucy stood in front of her mirror. Her body felt still and calm. She spoke her words to the Lucy looking back at her:

> "I have my plan.
> I have the skill.
> Yes I can.
> Yes I will."

The morning sun shone through the window and illuminated her reflection. She smiled at her changing self. "And a very good morning to you, Mr Blackbird," she said as she turned to greet her loyal visitor. But, a small, curious frown creased her brow when she saw that the branches outside were empty. *I could have sworn I heard him singing*, she muttered to herself. She paused in contemplation, before shaking her head with a questioning smile and heading downstairs.

Grandma Roberts was having breakfast with Rita today, so Lucy chose to skip hers. She headed straight to what used to be Grandma's 'storage' room. Really, that was just a fancy name for her 'I'm-not-sure-where-to-put-this' room. *Just one more look before Molly gets here,* she thought gleefully. She slowly opened the door and allowed her gaze to fall across the newly painted walls, the magazine–strewn shelves and the boxes of sparkly sequins and rainbow-coloured buttons. It was now her and Molly's *clothing design studio*! She breathed in a deep, contented sigh and gave herself a well-earned hug.

Her daydream-trance was broken by a cheery '*rat-tat-tat-tat*' *on the door – That must be Molly.*

A more-excited-than-usual Molly was already spinning into the hallway before Lucy had chance to even fully open the door,

63

let alone utter a *'hello'*. She looked at her friend in amusement. "What's that?" she asked with a smile, directing her gaze to the small case Molly was clutching.

"You'll never believe it!" answered Molly. "Mum has only gone and found us a sewing machine! It was really weird. Apparently, she was up in the loft looking for some old photos when she uncovered it. She didn't know it was even up there," Molly added in disbelief.

Lucy smiled a large smile. "I know exactly where we can put that!" she said as she took the case from Molly. The girls headed to their *studio*, and Lucy placed it proudly on what they now called their *Design Desk*. "How lucky are we?" she breathed.

But Molly was too busy circling the room in wonder. "Wow, Lucy!*"* she declared admiringly. "You've really worked hard on this since I was last here. It looks amazing!'"

Lucy looked at her friend. "It's not quite finished yet though," she said with an excited grin. "We are missing one important piece of the puzzle," she teased as Molly slowly nodded in understanding.

"Clothes!" they both cried in unison. "Time to go shopping!" they sang as they held each other's hands and danced around in a circle.

Molly suddenly stopped. "Hmmm," she pondered. "How are we actually going to get the clothes?"

"We'll find a way," answered Lucy with certainty. She searched her active mind for a solution. "A-ha!" she announced. "Got it," she shouted over her shoulder as she disappeared out of the door. Molly waited, intrigued, as she listened to Lucy's footsteps pitter-patter up, and back down the stairs.

Lucy returned holding a purple piggy bank. "We thought we wouldn't be able to afford them," she said with bright enthusiasm. "But, if we use some of my savings and go rummaging in charity shops, I think we'll be able to get all sorts of different items for hardly any money!"

"Genius idea!" said Molly as she high-fived her friend. "I've got a bit of pocket-money in my purse as well, so we can use that too."

"OK then! Let's go shopping for the Lolly Label range," squealed Molly. They both giggled as they remembered the fun they had had coming up with the name for their designs. They knew they wanted to use a combination of their names, and both agreed that 'Lolly' sounded way better than 'Mucy'!

The eager friends quickly grabbed their bags and coats, and ran to the door. Molly abruptly stopped as she caught sight of her reflection in the hallway mirror. "Hang on," she said to Lucy. "I just need to put my lip gloss on."

Lucy playfully wrapped her arms around Molly and gave her a reassuring squeeze. "Nah," she said dismissively. "It'll only wipe off when we have our hot chocolates." She then pointed to Molly's reflection. "And, see her?" she asked. Molly nodded. "Well, she is beautiful with or without her lip gloss anyway."

Molly grinned playfully, confidently opened the door and flicked her hair behind her shoulder. "Yeah!" she responded happily. "You're right." And they stepped out into the sunshine to begin the day's adventure.

The girls linked arms and happily skipped along the pavement. Lucy began to sing her new song in time with their steps – *'I have a plan, I have the skill, yes I can, yes I will!'* "What's that song?" Molly asked. "I love it!"

"Haha! It's my new tune. I made it up. It makes me smile and helps me through my wobbly days, you know, those days when your leaf boat gets stuck?" Lucy explained.

"Yeah, I sure do," answered Molly, but she was soon distracted by the sight of a charity shop. "Oooo! Let's go in there," she suggested eagerly, and the girls walked, wide-eyed, into the store.

"Wouldn't it be cool if charity shops did sale items?" Molly mused.

"What, like that 50p basket over there!" Lucy said with a grin, and pointed to a large bin brimming with clothes.

"No way!" cried Molly. "What are the chances?" The delighted friends skipped across and started rummaging through their lucky treasure-find.

"How about you look for accessories, Luce," suggested Molly. "You're so good at that! And I'll look for outfits," she added.

"Definitely!" agreed Lucy. "You're always really creative and good at putting different items together."

Lucy held up a pair of shoes. "I think these would be great for our fashion show that we're doing for Ruth and Grandma Roberts," she said excitedly.

Molly began to giggle. "Yeah," she said teasingly. "And it looks like they'll even fit your big feet," she added in jest.

"Haha!" answered Lucy with a smile. "You know how much I love my big feet! If they were any smaller, I'd blow over in a big gust of wind! And these two beauties," she continued as she looked down admiringly at her feet, "are going to get me exactly where I need to go."

After some very happy and eager delving, the girls finally scooped up all of their chosen bargains and carried them across to the shop counter.

"Hi, girls," greeted the shop assistant with a friendly smile. "It looks like you've found some lovely items today."

"Yes!" agreed Lucy, taking out her purse.

"We're fashion designers," interjected Molly, enjoying how amazing it was to say these words, and how grown-up they sounded. "We're getting ready for our first fashion show!" she offered excitedly. "It's only for our family though."

"Well, big dreams have to start somewhere," said the assistant wisely. "But small seeds of ideas can grow into big trees! And at least you're planting those seeds, girls. Good luck!" she said kindly. "I am sure you will be a great success."

Lucy and Molly turned and walked out of the shop, giggling and stumbling under the weight of their inspired purchases. Lucy linked arms with her dear friend. But she suddenly sighed and gazed thoughtfully at nothing in particular. "I so wish Mum could be here to see what we're up to," she said reflectively.

Molly gently squeezed Lucy's arm in understanding – a small but hugely meaningful gesture; words were not needed in that moment between the two friends.

All of a sudden, an unexpected gust of wind blew around their legs and rustled their bags. It whipped up a pile of leaves that had settled at their feet. Something caught Lucy's eye. She looked down to watch the breeze seemingly pick out a particular leaf, lift it off the ground and reveal a bright, shiny penny beneath it. Lucy stopped.

Molly's gaze was drawn to what Lucy was staring at. "Hey! How cool!" she exclaimed. "See a penny pick it up, all day long you'll have good luck," she chanted.

There was an abrupt moment of stillness as the girls stopped and slowly looked at each other in questioning wonder: *Mum?*

"Nah, that's just a coincidence, surely" said Lucy, shaking her head a little.

Molly smirked. "Are you sure?"

* Sarah *

As the sun rose on a chilly, crisp morning at the farm, Sarah pulled her coat tight around her. She cringed as she heard a distinctive ripping sound. What had started as a small hole the night before obviously had much bigger ideas for itself now. The cool air whirled around and into her clothes as she leant forwards to stroke the injured sheep by her feet. She desperately fought her eyelids which were trying so hard to close and let some much needed sleep in. Sarah quickly shook her head and tapped her icy cheeks: *Come on, stay awake!* She leant back against the hay bale behind her, but soon became restless. She jumped up to check the water bucket and rearrange the sheep's straw-bed, despite having done it just five minutes before. "At least you'll be nice and warm in your woolly jumper," she said soothingly to her four-legged companion.

Sarah looked wilfully at her woollen patient and began to hum her little tune:

> "I have my plan.
> I have the skill.
> Yes you can.
> Yes you will."

She had sung this song many times before to herself. It made the lonely nights under her duvet seem, somehow, less lonely, and she wanted now to share it with her new friend. "It's going to be all right, Mrs Sheep," she murmured tenderly. "You'll soon be back out in the field with all your friends."

A rustling sound behind her suddenly pulled Sarah out of the little love-cocoon she had built around her and the sheep. She glanced sleepily over her shoulder, expecting to see Aunt Lily or one of the dogs, but there was no one there. *Hmmm*, she thought to herself. *I could have sworn I heard somebody.*

"Hello," she called into the chilly air, but there was no response. Sarah couldn't help but smile to herself at the thought of there being a 'not-quite-there', mystery visitor. As she contemplated this intriguing idea, the warmth of the rising sun warmed her frosty skin, and she could fight sleep no more.

"Ahem," coughed Mr McGever. Sarah stirred in her little straw-nest and opened her sleepy eyes. She was greeted by the welcome sight of a large, steaming mug of hot chocolate and a bacon sandwich. Her mouth watered.

"I thought you'd be ready for this, young lass," said Mr McGever kindly. "Your Aunt Lily just told me that you've been out here all night after the evening's events!"

Sarah hoisted her weary body up. She took the sandwich gratefully from Mr McGever and tucked in greedily. A little nod was all she could manage to express her thanks.

As her little body started to absorb the welcome food, she began to update Mr McGever, through hungry mouthfuls. "Yeah," she confirmed. "Poor Mrs Sheep got her leg caught in some fencing and then panicked and she has cut it really bad, but Uncle Fergus said that a bandage and some rest is what she needs. And I couldn't leave her on her own," she added matter-of-factly, before taking a huge gulp of hot chocolate.

"Well, that was good of you, lass," said Mr McGever admiringly. "I am sure the sheep will be just fine now, thanks to you."

Sarah smiled shyly at the compliment.

"OK, I think whilst you finish your breakfast, I'll go and get some fresh bandages," Mr McGever said decisively. "And maybe you could help me redress her leg?" he asked as he took off his hat and ruffled his hair.

Sarah gave him an enthusiastic, bacon-y thumbs up.

Mr McGever quickly returned and promptly passed a black bag to Sarah. "I forgot all about this," he said. "I've just found it whilst I was getting the bandages. I reckon you could make good use of it."

"What is it, Mr McG?" Sarah asked with uninhibited curiosity.

"Have a look," answered Mr McGever. "It's an animal first aid kit," he explained as he knelt down and began to unwind the old bandage from the sheep's leg. "Oh, by the way," he added. "Don't forget, it's Thursday. Your Aunt Lily and Uncle Fergus will be picking up supplies in town and you'll be at mine, like usual."

Sarah gave a vague nod to acknowledge the reminder, but was far too captivated by her new case and its contents. "Thank you! I promise to take good care of it, Mr McG!" she breathed with glowing pride.

"Right, enough of that rummaging," instructed Mr McGever. "Come across here and help with this new bandage, would you, lass?"

Sarah was only too happy to oblige.

Mr McGever directed his new assistant. "You start at the top and make your way down," he instructed. "And you wrap it round as you go." He watched the eager young girl before him – eyes focused, brow furrowed in concentration, hands busy at their task. "We've got a vet in the making here, I reckon," he acknowledged with a wink. "That'll do for now then," he said. "Let's leave her to rest and she'll be back out in the field in no time."

Mr McGever set to collecting all the old bandages and tidying the make-shift hospital bed. He turned to inform Sarah that it was time to go but found a very stern-faced little madam staring back at him with lips pursed and hands on hips. He suppressed a smirk. "What is it, lass?" he asked in amusement.

"Mrs Sheep needs to go back with her friends now!" Sarah asserted. "She is supposed to be in a flock, not on her own, Mr McG!" she added, with more insistence than a nine-year-old should have.

Mr McGever cheekily mimicked Sarah by placing his hands on his hips and pouting. "Now, now, Miss Impatient," he pretend-warned with a grin. "There is something called 'the right time', you know. And when the sheep is ready to go back into the field, she'll let us know when that time is. We have to wait for the green light from her before we put her back where she belongs. It's not for us to decide. You see, Sarah," he continued wisely. "You need to let things unfold in their own time. If you try and do things before that 'right time', you'll make the job twice as hard." He was speaking from years of experience…and a few mistakes!

Sarah knew this was not a point to be argued with and began to follow Mr McGever out of the barn.

"Whoah there, lass," said Mr McGever. "What on earth happened to your coat?" he asked with concern as he inspected the now widening tear.

Sarah peered down at the gaping hole to which he was referring. "Oh, I just caught it on the fence when I was helping to get Mrs Sheep out," she explained dismissively.

Mr McGever smiled a self-satisfied smile as he briskly walked across to his truck and retrieved a bag from the back seat. "Perfect timing then," he said with a touch of mysticism, and he handed the package to Sarah.

"Another present?" asked Sarah with bright, eager eyes.

"Well, now that you're a proper country girl, you'll need a proper country coat. One that can cope with those all-nighters," said Mr McGever. "I'm pretty sure that won't be your last," he added with a wink.

Sarah lifted a thick, tweed jacket out of the bag. She immediately wriggled out of her torn coat, flung it aside and pulled on her new one. She twirled round and around. "Thank you so much, Mr McG," she cried. "I love it," she added with immense gratitude…and a huge grin.

"Come on, you," urged Mr McGever lovingly. "Let's get you back and warmed up." The tall farmer with the big heart draped his arm around his little companion's shoulders and they made their way, in comfortable silence, to his truck. A short time later the wheels of the truck splashed through the puddles of the McGever farm, announcing their arrival. One of the farm workers waved as Mr McGever slowed the vehicle and wound down the window. "Everything all right, John?" Mr McGever asked his friend.

"Yes, mate," answered John reassuringly. "The tractor's running like a charm since you added that new part."

"Thanks, John. Good to know," replied Mr McGever as he pulled off and directed the truck towards the house.

"What does he do, Mr McG?" enquired Sarah quizzically.

"Well, lass," answered Mr McGever. "John does the ploughing. And Tom over there," he added, pointing to another

70

of the farm employees. "He does the cows. And me and Brody do mechanics and help your Aunt Lily and Uncle Fergus with their sheep," he explained.

"Hmmm," said Sarah with a contemplative frown. "That sounds like something my daddy was telling me. Something about the 'Abba' something 'knees'," she tried to explain, scratching her head.

As Mr McGever pulled his truck into the turning circle in front of the farmhouse and turned off the engine, he turned to his confused, little passenger. "You'll have to explain a bit better than that, lass," he said with a frown.

"Well, there were these people, like a family, and they all did what they were best at. Everyone had a different job, I think. Well, it was something like that. I can't really remember," she said, a little baffled.

They both climbed out of the truck and began to make their way inside. Once in the kitchen, Mr McGever set to making lunch, whilst quietly searching for meaning in Sarah's words. He suddenly stopped as inspiration dawned, like a lighthouse beam illuminating a hidden treasure chest on a beach. "Oh!" he said to Sarah. "I think you're talking about the Aborigines!" he exclaimed. "Head over to that bookcase, and you'll find a red book on the second shelf. Go grab it for me, please, lass," Mr McGever said as he busied himself with carrots and potatoes.

Sarah walked across and scanned the second shelf. As her gaze settled on a book she knew so well, she suddenly gasped and her little hands flew to her mouth. She slowly slid the red book out, hardly daring to look, but desperate to look, all at the same time. She was right! It was the exact book that her daddy had had. *Daddy?* Sarah galloped back to Mr McGever. "This is it! This is it!" she cried, hardly able to contain her excitement. "This is the same book my daddy had!"

"Huh," answered Mr McGever. "What a coincidence…"

"Are you sure?" whispered Sarah.

Unconditional Love

Lucy

The tea was flowing, the laughter was light and the chat was cheery. Ruth and Grandma Roberts were having one of their much-loved catch-ups at Mrs Roberts's house. But they were suddenly interrupted, mid-sentence, by the sound of the key in the front door. Molly and Lucy were back. The next moment was a flurry of rustling bags, crashing doors, falling shoes, jangling keys and, of course, giggling teenagers. Ruth and Grandma Roberts exchanged a smile: *Guess they're home then.*

"We're in the kitchen," called Ruth. The girls skipped through to join the older women and plonked their many bags down onto the table. Ruth and Grandma Roberts only just had time to lift their cups of tea out of the way before there was an unfortunate liquid-y accident. The girls, apparently oblivious to this near-miss, promptly tipped their precious finds all over the table. It was soon a sea of bright accessories and flowing materials.

"Hang on a minute, girls," instructed Ruth. "Just before you show us these amazing purchases, I'd like to share something with Lucy." Ruth glanced at Molly with a knowing smile and a twinkle in her eye. Molly pressed her lips together, trying to hold in the secret that wanted so desperately to escape. She placed her hand firmly over her mouth: an extra seal over her excitement. She felt like a volcano just gearing up to a monumental eruption.

Before Ruth was able to utter a single word, the sunlight streaming through the window glinted off something on her hand. Lucy gasped in delight as she realised it was a diamond ring, settled comfortably in its new home on Ruth's left ring-finger. Molly could not contain herself a moment longer and she leapt over to Lucy. The girls twirled and squealed and bounced their way around the kitchen. Ruth was just about to open her mouth to speak but quickly changed her mind. There was no point trying to talk above the girl's screams of excitement. She settled back in her chair, cradled her cup of tea and waited for the volume to come down at least a little bit. This could take a while!

Grandma Roberts rolled her eyes and pretended to look at her watch. "Whenever you're ready, girls," she said cheekily. "Sometime this week would be nice, so Ruth can actually tell you the full story." The girls paused but then caught each other's eyes and the squealing began all over again. Ruth and Grandma Roberts shook their heads in resignation.

"I'll make us a fresh pot," she said to Ruth with a chuckle. "You might be waiting some time yet."

Ruth smiled and leant down to lift a wedding magazine from her bag. She began idly flicking through the pages, faking disinterest in the frenzied spectacle before her, a small smirk on her face.

After what seemed like an inordinate amount of time, a sense of calm descended on the kitchen once again. Well, it was almost a sense of calm. Ruth paused, just to make sure, and then finally began her story. "Lucy, you have probably guessed already, thanks to my not so discreet daughter here, that Luke proposed to me in the most magical way. But, more of that later. For now, I'd like you both just to sit down a moment as I have a question to ask you first."

Lucy and Molly exchanged a quizzical glance and pulled out a chair each. They lowered themselves into their seats, but did not take their wide, hopeful eyes off Ruth for a single second. Grandma Roberts returned to the table with fresh tea...and the special biscuits.

Ruth continued. "Girls, you know how much I love your clothing design ideas. Well, I was wondering if Lolly Label would consider designing my bridesmaids dresses and working alongside the tailor who is making my wedding dress?"

The room stayed momentarily silent as the tantalising question hung in the air like a kite flying high on an uplifting thermal. But the words slowly filtered through and the volcano erupted once again. Ruth waved her hands at the bouncing duo to try and hold their attention for just a few seconds longer. "I haven't finished yet," said Ruth intriguingly. "I have one more question." The girls held their breath. "Would you two be my chief bridesmaids? And would you wear your Lolly Label designs on my special day?"

Lucy couldn't hold the building emotion in a single second longer, and tears started to cascade down her cheeks…tears of pure joy. Molly squeezed her friend's hand…she knew only too well how important this was for her, on so many levels. And she was, of course, excited for herself too. Lucy looked down and tried to collect her thoughts but the emotion took over, and she let it. For the first time in a very long time, she dared to hope that things were going to get better. Ruth instinctively wrapped her arms around both Molly and Lucy, hugging her girls close. "I think we are all ready to start to celebrate love once more," she whispered with happiness.

Molly suddenly pulled away from the group-hug. Her excitement and impatience had other ideas! "Come on, Lucy!" she said eagerly. "Let's go and start designing our dresses!" she suggested. Without waiting for an answer, she peeled Lucy off Ruth and dragged her to their design studio. Lucy quickly wiped her tears and bounded after her friend.

Ruth glanced across at Grandma Roberts. "Well, I think it's safe to say that went well," she said with a large, beaming smile. Grandma Roberts laughed and nodded enthusiastically in agreement.

"For a few weeks now," said Grandma Roberts, "I have been seeing Lucy as a little snowdrop trying desperately to make its way through the frozen soil. And I think today is the first day I can definitely say that she might have just made it. My little flower is now blooming." She swallowed down the tears and shifted uncomfortably in her seat. She swiftly changed the subject, eager to move on from this emotionally-charged conversation. "Anyway, Ruth," she said with a small cough, "how are you getting on with Something Old, Something New, Something Borrowed, Something Blue, love?" she enquired with interest.

"I've got everything apart from Something Borrowed," answered Ruth.

"Well, you have plenty of time yet, dear," Grandma Roberts said reassuringly.

Whilst Molly flicked excitedly through the pages in Ruth's wedding magazine, Lucy stood in the doorway, listening to the unfolding conversation between Ruth and her Grandma. She glanced thoughtfully at her wooden box and a small idea began to take shape in her mind. But, she was abruptly distracted by a beaming Molly thrusting a pencil and a piece of paper at her. "Come on, design partner! Let's get drawing," she instructed.

A short while later, Ruth opened the door of the studio to find the girls sitting happily in a sea of paper, pencils, silk, magazines and ribbons. "Molly," she said. "Come on, love. It's time for us to be heading off now." She scanned the scene in front of her. "Wow! It looks like you two are making progress already," she said admiringly.

"We are, Mum," answered Molly elatedly. "We'll have them finished in no time! You'll see!" she added with unreserved delight.

"Well, perhaps you could come round tomorrow night, after school, to carry on with your designs," suggested Ruth. Molly reluctantly dragged herself to her feet. She did not want to leave at all but knew this wasn't up for discussion with Ruth.

"See you tomorrow, Luce," Molly said with an exaggerated pout as she exited the room.

"Ruth?" Lucy said slowly as she too rose to her feet.

"Yes, love," answered Ruth warmly.

Lucy glanced down at her feet, suddenly feeling very shy and nervous. "I just wanted to…um…say thank you, you know, for asking me to be…err…part of your special day," she muttered self-consciously.

Ruth walked across and hugged Lucy tightly. "It wouldn't be even half as special without you there, love," she answered tenderly. She was just about to leave but sensed Lucy still had something she wanted to say. She looked at her encouragingly.

Lucy knelt down next to her box, lifted the lid and reached inside. She took out the white, leather purse that had held Penny's wedding ring and peeked at Ruth. "Maybe this could be your Something Borrowed," she offered quietly. "It was my mum's wedding-ring purse." Ruth hurried to kneel by Lucy's side as tears welled up in her eyes.

"Oh, Lucy," she breathed. "I don't know what to say. I would be honoured. Thank you! Your mum would be so proud of you."

The wedding day finally arrived. The church was silhouetted against the blue sky and the sun overlooked the beautiful scene. Ruth waited nervously in the entrance – the grand wooden doors stood like loyal friends by her side. She made a few last adjustments to her dress and took in a big, steadying breath. Her dad offered his arm for her to link with and kissed his daughter proudly on the forehead. Lucy lifted the train of Ruth's wedding dress to smooth out the last of the creases. She exchanged a nervous but thrilled look with Molly. They both giggled and winked a secret code at each other.

It was time. A mild breeze rustled the leaf-spectators in the trees and the gentle symphony of the organ drifted out of the doors. Lucy took the first step inside. She took a moment to absorb her surroundings – the church filled with flowers; Ruth so beautiful in her wedding dress; Luke waiting proudly at the end of the aisle; and her stunning, self-designed dress. She was suddenly transported back to the day she was sitting at the kitchen table with her dear family, and she could hear her mum's words as clearly as if she was standing there, right by her side…"'HOPE' is the feeling that will help you to believe that you can be or do or have anything you want. But you must hold tight to that belief in yourself. It's more than OK to hope for something to come true. And it's definitely OK to believe that it *will* come true, even when it is a baby-dream only just starting to take shape in your head."

Lucy's body began to tingle and the hairs on her arms stood up as a shiver of realisation ran down her spine: *Mum, you were right. Dreams really do come true. But how we get there may always be the most incredible mystery.*

* Sarah *

Sarah stood, wide-eyed in the McGever farm kitchen, still holding the red book protectively but lovingly to her chest. She stood for a moment, simply watching. Mr McGever was making tea, and Brody was playing in the other room. An unexplainable feeling began to stir inside her tummy. She didn't have a word for it, but it was similar to the feeling she used to have at home with Lucy, and her mum and dad. She willingly let it in, this long-lost sensation.

But she was suddenly pulled from her daydream by Brody, who entered the kitchen, noisily pulled out a chair and nervously sat in it. He looked fidgety and restless, and started tapping his fingers impatiently on the table. Sarah's curiosity grew as she watched him squirm in his seat and glare purposefully at his dad. This was such unusual behaviour for Brody. *What was going on?*

Mr McGever took the not-very-subtle cue from his son and brought his cup of tea over to the table. He took a seat and motioned for Sarah to do the same. He winked at Brody and cleared his throat. "Right, young lass," he directed at a very intrigued Sarah. "Me and Brody have got something that we want to talk to you about."

Sarah had never seen him look this serious and she instinctively looked towards the back door, wondering if she should run now or wait to hear what he could possibly have to say that had got both him and Brody so jittery.

The huge smile that was now starting to spread across Brody's face told her that it might be worth sticking around to listen. *What is he so happy about?* she wondered, and her interest began to stir. She leaned just a tiny bit further forwards and intertwined her little fingers on the table.

"Well, me and Brody have…err…got a really important…um, question to ask you?" sputtered Mr McGever. "But, we don't need an answer right away, lass. You can take as much time as you like, and ask as many questions as you want," he added.

"Come on, Dad!" interjected Brody impatiently. "Just ask her already!" he instructed, rolling his eyes playfully and squirming excitedly in his chair.

Sarah looked expectantly at them both. "Ask me what!?" she questioned in bemusement.

"OK," said Mr McGever before steadying himself in his chair. "Would you like to be part of this family?" he blurted out, unable to hold back the large smile now taking over his face.

Sarah tilted her head in confusion, a little disappointed that all this build up had led to what she thought was a bit of a lame question. "I thought I was part of this family," she said quizzically.

Mr McGever chuckled his unmistakable chuckle and shook his head. "No, what I mean, lass, is…"

Brody couldn't take his dad's faffing any longer. He leapt to his feet and asked in a loud, clear voice, "Will you be my sister for ever and ever?!"

Silence.

Mr McGever was grateful for his son's frankness, which helped him find his voice too.

"What we mean, Sarah, is that we, well, technically, 'I', would like to adopt you, so you can become a forever-part of this family," he said, hoping he had chosen the right words.

Sarah sat in stunned shock. "What?" she asked in astonishment. "You mean this would be my new home and you would be my new dad and Brody would be my brother?" she continued, astonished by the sound and enormity of her own questions.

"Yes, lass," confirmed Mr McGever. "That's exactly what we mean. But you don't have to call me Dad. Your dad will always be George. But, if you'd like, I want to look after you and for you to be part of this family, and live with us," he explained.

A small shadow suddenly darkened Sarah's face. "But, what about Aunt Lily?" she asked, suddenly feeling a little unsure.

"Don't worry," reassured Mr McGever. "I've spoken with Lily and she wholeheartedly agrees that this is a great idea. Of course, she will miss you terribly, but she wants you to be happy, and I think we've both had enough of Brody going on and on about how much he wants to have you as his sister!" Mr McGever raised his eyebrows cheekily at his son, who shuffled his feet uncomfortably and mumbled something about that not quite being the truth. But his blushing cheeks defied him and told a completely different story.

Sarah leapt off her chair, marched straight to Mr McGever, jumped onto his lap and flung her arms around his neck. "I really want you to be my new dad!" she agreed eagerly. Mr McGever let out a large sigh and wrapped his arms around this little girl who had so captured his heart. "I was hoping you'd say that," he whispered.

Sarah soon felt an insistent tug at her arm. It was Brody. "Come on!" he said enthusiastically. "Let me show you your new room."

Sarah sat up and surprised Mr McGever with a big kiss on the cheek, before running off and disappearing up the stairs with Brody.

"Well," said Mr McGever decisively to the empty room. "I guess I had better make a phone call to Mrs Grey then, seeing as she is the one who has helped put all of this in place." His heart filled with love and delight as he reached into his pocket for his phone.

***

The day finally arrived. Sarah was up unusually early, gladly busying herself with packing suitcases and bags, and dragging them downstairs with a satisfying, *thump, thump, thump*. Mr McGever took them out to his awaiting truck. Sarah walked across to Lily, who was standing by the Aga, and wrapped her arms around her. Lily crouched down to better hug this little girl who had made such a huge impression on all of them. "Thank you, Aunt Lily," whispered Sarah.

Lily tucked a disobedient piece of hair behind Sarah's ear. "You will always be welcome here, Sarah," Lily stated warmly with a growing lump in her throat. "But I could not be more pleased that you have found exactly where you belong."

Sarah smiled a huge grin. "Don't worry, Aunt Lily," she said. "I still have to help you with the sheep," she added over her shoulder as she ran out of the kitchen, grabbing her purple, spotty wellies.

She skipped her way excitedly across the yard, to Mr McGever's truck. Her little legs began to swing as she settled herself into the passenger seat and clicked her belt firmly in place. Mr McGever glanced across at Lily, who was now standing in the front doorway, and tipped his hat in her direction. A tiny gesture but one that spoke a thousand words between them. Lily wiped the tears unselfconsciously from her cheeks and watched the truck disappear down the driveway. She smiled to herself as she thought of her dear Penny: *It all worked out in the end for our Sarah, my dear friend. And I just know you'd be standing here waving her off to this new life, with a big grin on your face too.*

Mr McGever's truck bounced its way through the puddles and into his farm. Brody ran out of the door at an impressive speed and straight to the back of the truck. He yanked the door open and began excitedly hauling Sarah's bags out.

"Hang on there, son!" chuckled Mr McGever. "Let me at least stop the truck first!" he instructed good-naturedly as he turned off the ignition with a satisfied sigh. Sarah leapt out and went immediately to the boot too, to retrieve her wooden box. She and Brody ran inside and raced straight upstairs, chattering excitedly about this and that. Neither gave even a tiny backwards glance. This present moment was exactly where they wanted to be.

Mr McGever stepped out of his truck just as a hire car pulled into the driveway and up alongside him. He bent slightly to get a better look at his visitor. The car door opened and out stepped Mrs Grey. "You must be Mr McGever," she said amiably. "It's lovely to finally meet you." She stretched a little and leaned down to straighten her pleated, beige skirt.

"Same to you," responded Mr McGever warmly, as he reached out to shake Mrs Grey's hand. "Sarah has told me all about you. She sure is excited to show you this place." Mr McGever gestured for her to follow him inside. "I'll make some tea," he said with a smile.

Sarah and Brody were still busy upstairs, playing house-movers. Brody was attempting to unpack one of the suitcases but really he was just moving stuff from one part of the room to the other. Sarah placed her wooden box on her new bed and took out Dandelion-Horse. She kissed him lovingly on the nose and placed him in prime position on the window sill. "There you go, Dandelion," she murmured. "I think you're going to like our new home. Look at all those fields out there!"

They were suddenly interrupted by the sound of Mr McGever speaking with somebody downstairs. Sarah and Brody both paused and listened, trying to place the lady's voice they could now hear. Then Sarah had a light-bulb moment of recognition, and she tripped out of the room and sprinted down the stairs, in true Sarah style.

"Where are you going?" enquired Brody after her.

"To say thank you to Mrs Grey!" she yelled back over her shoulder. "She's the one who made all this come true!"

Sarah ran straight into the kitchen and straight into Mrs Grey's arms. "Thank you, thank you, thank you, Mrs Grey," Sarah cried with unrestrained gratitude.

Mrs Grey shuffled uneasily and patted Sarah awkwardly on the back. "Well now," she stuttered. "You're...um, very welcome little...err...one," she continued self-consciously. "It was...um...my pleasure." Sarah was happily oblivious to the older lady's embarrassment.

Mr McGever thought now might be a good time to rescue poor Mrs Grey from her struggle with this little girl's open warmth. "Come on, young lass," he said with a sly smile. "We have one last surprise for you."

"Another one?" asked Sarah in wonder as Brody slid expertly into the kitchen and headed straight for the boot rack.

"I'll show you, Sarah!" he cried gleefully as he led the way outside – the Pied Piper followed by an excited little girl, a tall, proud farmer and an edgy woman in a pleated, beige skirt.

The unlikely group made their way towards a grassy field at the back of the house. It was a few minutes before the larger members caught up with the more agile, smaller ones. Sarah watched in wonderment as Brody stopped at a metal gate and picked up a bucket of nuts. He shook it vigorously and the rattle-y sound echoed around the valley. There was a moment of breath-held silence. All of a sudden, the faint sound of hooves broke the stillness and eight curious eyes looked towards the far end of the field. It wasn't long before the owner of the sound could be seen! A beautiful pony cantered effortlessly up over the brow of the meadow and straight to the gate. "Hello," greeted Brody as he held out his nut-filled hand. The horse tucked in, greedily.

Sarah was in awe! She stroked its white blaze and gazed into its eyes. "He's so beautiful," she gasped with breathless admiration. "What's his name?" she asked, not taking her eyes of the pony for one second. She was a little girl in love.

"Well," answered Mr McGever. "That's for the owner to decide."

"Oh, OK," said Sarah. "So, who is the owner?" she asked as she turned to face Mr McGever.

"You are!" Brody said simply.

Sarah's eyes instantly filled with tears of pure delight. "Really, Mr McG?" she sobbed.

Mr McGever nodded and smiled. "He's all yours, young lass," he confirmed. "Chores and all," he added teasingly. Sarah ran across and jumped straight into his arms.

It was all too much for the little girl who had endured so much. "Thank you so very lots and lots," she wept, and buried her face into Mr McGever's neck.

It wasn't long before Brody got fed up with all the girlie theatrics. "So, Sarah," he interrupted, "what's his name?" he asked impatiently.

Sarah looked up and gazed at her stunning new animal-friend. She didn't need to think this one through at all. She took in a large breath. "Dandelion," she whispered.

There wasn't much that was going to be able to drag Sarah away from Dandelion's side today, but she had a sudden thought. "I can't wait to tell Lucy!" she cried. "Can I call her now, Mr McG?" she asked.

"Of course you can, lass," answered Mr McGever easily. "You know where the phone is."

Sarah leapt out of his arms and bounced back to the farm. She spun into the kitchen, grabbed the phone and frantically typed in Grandma Robert's number.

"Hello?" said a familiar voice at the other end of the line.

"Lucy! It's me!" cried Sarah. "You'll never guess what?" But before Lucy even had chance to ask, Sarah was in full flow. "So, you know today is the day I am starting to live with Mr McG and Brody? Well, he got me a pony, Lucy! My very own pony! He's called Dandelion and he's so beautiful!" she squealed. Lucy absorbed her baby sister's incredible news and patiently waited for Sarah's motor-mouth to slow down.

Sarah finally caught her breath and Lucy grasped her moment. "Well, Sarah. Do you remember what Mum said in the kitchen that day?" she asked. "'HOPE' is the feeling that will help you to believe that you can be or do or have anything you want. But you must hold tight to that belief in yourself. It's more than OK to hope for something to come true. And it's definitely OK to believe that it *will* come true, even when it is a baby-dream only just starting to take shape in your head."

Sarah looked around her new home, and a huge grin lit up her whole face. She held the phone closer to her ear to better absorb her big sister's words of wisdom, as she had so often done with her mum. A little thought began to stir: *Mummy, you were right. Dreams really do come true.*

Part 2
Activity Book

Contents

Activity Book

Hi Reader,

It's Lucy and Sarah here! Woohoo!!! Well done if you have got this far. That means that we have been on this whole epic journey, together! We are so excited and so proud of you for reaching this point! Totally cool! You are awesome!

We are so happy that you could come on our journey with us, but now we are even more thrilled to go on your journey of discovery with you.

So, who was your favourite character? Was it one of us? Perhaps it was the big, friendly giant, Mr McGever? Or maybe one of Sarah's four-legged friends?

Anyway, are you ready to start your activities now? We hope so!

As you may have noticed whilst reading our story, every journey starts with a single step. That's all – just one, and it doesn't even need to be a big one. Cool, right? Hang on a minute…we don't mean like an actual journey, like going on a bus somewhere. We mean the whole adventure of your life. We know that sounds a bit like something a grown-up might go on about. We didn't really get it at first. But, you will. So, what we have done for you, is put together an Activity Book, packed with all our favourites. With each activity you complete, you get one step closer to discovering the hidden treasure inside you. The magic is waiting for you! Just like it was waiting for us.

In every chapter, we learnt a new lesson in life, you know, something that really got us thinking – something really real that stuck with us. Sometimes it was easy, but sometimes it was soooooo hard! We're actually wondering – have you already figured out what some of those lessons were?

However, along the way there were always people around to help us, like family, friends or animals. The most important bit, is not to give up or stop believing in yourself. We almost did a few times, but we're so glad we didn't!

You might want to do some of the activities with your family, some on your own or some with your friends or a keyworker or nanny. Sometimes you might be able to get started straight away, but sometimes you might only be able to make a plan with somebody and then do your activity later. It's all cool. We don't mind how the activities get done – just do them in a way that feels best to you and whoever you are doing them with. You don't need to rush any of this – it could take you a few weeks, or a year! It's up to you. There is no hand-in date, like with homework – hooray! If you finish every single activity though, you will be well on your way to making your box of dreams come true.

If you want to change any of the activities, we'd be cool with that too.

Oh, one last thing before we let you get on…always remember that this is *your* journey and that these are *your* dreams…so, GO BIG!

Lots of love,
Lucy and Sarah
XOXO

Activity 1: Box of Dreams

Hi guys,

It's Sarah here! Lucy and I have decided that we are going to take it in turns to go through all the different activities with you. I am so flippin' excited! We thought it would be best to start at the very beginning. Good place to begin, right? Do you remember in the first chapter of the story, me and Lucy were playing in the attic with our box, and Lucy was talking about marriage and kissing? Yuk!!!

Well, we want you to be able to have as much fun as we had with our, 'What-I-Want-To-Be-When-I-Grow-Up' box, so let's make yours! Are you ready? Of course you are…

1) Time to go on the hunt for: a box, jar or big sheet of paper;

2) Next, we need felt tip pens, lots and lots of stickers, ribbon, magazines – basically anything you can find to decorate your box, jar or sheet with (apart from mud, I tried it, and boy did it not turn out like I thought it would!);

3) Please place your left hand in the air and repeat after me – "I, (your name), promise to dream big, so massively big that even the adults will want to join in on my dreams.";

4) Write on post-it notes, draw on pieces of paper, cut out pictures and collect objects that are connected to your dreams! Just like my toy animals and Lucy's dolls. Put them in your box or jar, or decorate your paper with them. Oh, and if you are doing it all with pictures, stick the pictures of the things you want, the places you want to go and even the people you want to meet onto the paper, or put them in the box or jar;

5) Phew!!! Good job everyone! I love that sticking part and the cutting part and the other sticking part! Now, all that is left to do is find the best place ever to put your box/jar/paper. It should be somewhere you will see it every single day, so that you can remember and be transported into your future! Maybe some of it has already come true...

See you soon, guys!

Love,
Sarah x

Activity 2: Tribe Dream

Hey everybody,

It's Lucy here! I bet you enjoyed doing Sarah's first activity – it was cool wasn't it? Even though she is a totally annoying, nine-year-old, little sister! Haha! I wish I could see your box of dreams...or jar, or sheet – whichever you decided to use. I wonder what your biggest dream is. I wonder if it's a secret or if you have told somebody about it.

Anyway, I'm getting distracted. Sorry – you'll get used to that with me! So, here is my first activity. Do you remember when Sarah and I were sitting around the dinner table with Mum and Dad? Dad was teaching us all about the Aborigines? Sarah couldn't even say the word! Haha! Sisters!

Well, the main thing I learnt from Dad's story was that each person in the Aborigine tribe has a different job and that, in the end, this helps everybody. I don't think you'll need loads of sticky tape this time – maybe just a big piece of paper and some coloured pens (I LOVE coloured pens!).

OK – here is your activity:

1) First of all, think about who your tribe is. It could be your family at home or your group of friends at school or your team mates at a club you go to. It doesn't matter, but it has to be people you know pretty well and there has to be at least two members. Then draw each tribe member on the paper – I liked giving everybody weird hair-dos and funny clothes when I did this! You can use photos instead though, if you like;

2) Next, think about what your tribe's goal is, you know, what the BIG dream is for all of you, together. It could be anything, but it has to be something that you couldn't do alone. So, you know that my tribe dream is designing clothes with Molly? Well, this is definitely something I

need her for because she is good at things I'm not good at, and I'm good at things she isn't good at. And there is no way we could be doing the things we do if one of us wasn't there. So, your goal could be, for example, creating your own Sport's Team or selling cakes at school or putting a band together – it doesn't matter;

3) Now, you need to give everybody in the tribe their own, special job. Here, you need to really think about what each person is good at, what kind of personality they have and any cool talents they've got! If my tribe-dream had anything to do with animals, I would definitely give that job to Sarah – she is so good with them! Don't tell her I said that though!

Have fun with this activity! I bet you learn something about all the members that you didn't know before! Hopefully you can see that by all of you coming together as a tribe, you get to dream so much bigger! And you know how much Sarah and I LOVE dreaming!

Lots of love,
Lucy
xoxo

Activity 3: Being Thankful

OK! Get ready, set, Geronimo!!!

It's me, Sarah! Onto my next activity!

Do you remember when Lucy and I were just about to have dinner with Mum and Dad? And do you remember that I flicked water at Lucy when we were washing our hands? Tee-hee! Now that was a brilliant shot – well, I thought so anyway. Lucy still reminds me every single day about that! Oops! Ha! I was definitely in trouble that day, but even I know that when big people says it's time to settle down, I have to behave. Well, most of the time anyway!

Anyway, now, you'll need to get your family to join in with this activity, or whoever you have dinner with. If you don't want to do it at dinner with your family, that's OK. You could do it with other family members at another time, or with your keyworker at school. I now do this activity with my new family, Mr McG and Brody…and Dandelion, of course!

It's really simple:

1) Before you start your dinner, say something that you are thankful for. You know, something that happened that made you think, "Wow, I'm really glad that happened!" It can be something that happened that day or at another time – it doesn't matter;

2) Ask everyone else at the table to do the same. Woah, let me just clear something up here first – Dandelion doesn't actually come in and eat dinner with us!

3) Listen to what other people are grateful for too. I used to get really bored by this bit, but it's actually really cool to see what other people like. For example, the other night, Brody said he was thankful for me! Yes!!! Result!

That's it! This is a really easy one, but I like it. I can't quite put my finger on it, but there is something pretty magical about it. Everyone always ends up smiling, even Aunt Lily!

Over to you Lucy…

Love,
Sarah x

Activity 4: Your Dream

Hi – Lucy again!

I hope you liked my last activity. This next one is a little bit similar because it's all about dreaming again (woohoo!), but this time it's all about YOUR dream, you know, that one special dream that just belongs to you.

In this activity you get to make a map! And, you will most definitely need your coloured pens again! Yay!

If there is one thing Sarah and I both learnt on our journey, it's that you have to actually do something about reaching your dream – you can't just sit back and go, "Oh, it would be really cool if I was a singer in a band," and then just wait for it to happen. If there is going to be magic, there needs to be a magician! Hey! That's you!

Do you remember before Sarah got her pony, she had to do all kinds of smelly things with other horses, or was it sheep? Ewww! Either way, it was probably stinky! And before I turned Grandma Robert's room into a design studio for me and Molly, I was designing clothes for, and dressing up my dolls?

Basically, the point is, you've got to start somewhere! Oh yeah, that nice lady in the charity shop was talking about planting seeds and watching them grow into big trees, wasn't she? Awww – she was such a kind lady.

So, here is your activity – it's pretty simple, but definitely think carefully about your answers:

1)   Get a big piece of paper and your coloured pens. Draw a Dream Box on the right hand side of the page and then seven stepping stones which lead to the Dream Box (make sure they're big enough for you to write things in though). Decorate your map in a really cool way. You can use pictures, photos, drawings…anything really –

it's your map. When Molly and I did this activity we totally made our maps all about who we are;

2) Think about your special dream. What is it?
3) Once you have decided, write it in the Dream Box, on the map, at the end of the stepping-stones;
4) Next, think about what you can do to make YOUR dream come true. You need to come up with seven ideas and write them in the seven stepping stones. As always, you can write anything you want because this is YOUR dream.

If you're a bit stuck about what I mean, here's an example. First of all, I think it is way better to write things down that aren't too big. Only because I'm excited for you to get started straight away, so definitely write ideas down that you can get stuck into, now! So, for example, if it's your dream to be a chef, you probably don't want to put, "work with a world-famous chef in a world-famous restaurant." That might not be possible at our age! Haha! But, what might be cool is to find out if any family members or friends have any recipe books they no longer use, and perhaps start baking a few small things at home. You can then maybe have your family come to your kitchen 'restaurant' to be your taste-testers!

And there you have it…YOUR path to YOUR dream! Oh, I so wish I could see what you've written! It's so exciting!

Lots of love,
Lucy
xoxo

Activity 5: Feelings' Letter

Ah!!! You caught me!!! I was just having a go at Lucy's activities myself. For a big sister, she does have some pretty cool ideas, but don't tell her I said that!

So, do you remember when I was up in the attic, by myself, just before Aunt Lily came to collect me? I was just sitting there. I wanted to say so much but it felt like no one was listening to me, and that nobody cared about what I wanted. I was so sad and cross all at the same time. It wasn't exactly me behaving at my best, I must admit, but back then I didn't know things were going to turn out so good, and it was a pretty rubbish day.

Mum actually used to tell me that whenever I felt like that, I should write a letter to the person who I'm feeling sad about. She always said to be really honest in the letter, you know, really write down everything I was feeling and thinking. The cool bit though is that instead of giving the letter to that person, you either burn it on a fire or tear it into loads of tiny pieces. I did try this a few times and because it's really private, it meant I could tell that person exactly how I was feeling! It definitely helped. I never felt as cross afterwards.

Anyway, this next activity kind of goes with that. Here's what you do:

1. Get a piece of paper and a pen;
2. Write the name of the person who you are feeling sad or angry about at the top of the piece of paper, if you know it. It might be someone you know really well, or not. Or, it might be someone you saw on television, perhaps, who was doing something that made you angry or upset;
3. Write them a letter – it doesn't matter if it is one page or one hundred pages long. But you have to tell them everything you are feeling, what they have done, what

they haven't done and why you are so angry or sad. You get the idea;
4. Fold up the letter, put it in an envelope and seal it;
5. Throw it on your fire and burn it (you **definitely** need to ask permission from a grown-up for this bit). Or, if you don't have a fire, tear the letter up into as many tiny pieces as you can and throw it away.

That's it! But, like I said, man do I feel better once I have done it! It feels like I am getting every feeling inside of me that I don't want, out and onto the paper. It's cool!

OK, see you at the next activity...

Love,
Sarah x

Activity 6: Acts of Kindness

Hi Reader,

It's Lucy here again. I hope you're still having lots of fun with our activities! I am in coloured-pen heaven! I just love it! I used to spend hours sorting through my mum's catalogues and magazines, and organising Grandma Roberts's sewing box! I wonder what you like to spend hours doing…

I know what Sarah's answer would be…Dandelion, Dandelion, Dandelion! I mean, I guess Dandelion has kind of a cute face but you should smell Sarah's clothes after she's been riding or mucking in or is it 'mucking out'?… whatever you call it! Ewwwww!!

Anyway…look at me all distracted again! Told you! I had better get on with telling you about the next activity.

Here goes! So, this one is all about kindness. You know, really nice stuff that people do for other people. If I think about all the kind things that Grandma Roberts, Molly and Ruth have done for me, it makes me feel really smiley inside – kind of like that feeling you get when it's your birthday! Haha!

Do you remember when Molly invited me round for tea, and when Grandma Roberts let me turn her 'storage' room into my design studio? Well, that's what I'm talking about. Oh, and not forgetting when Sarah sent me my very own 'What-I-Want-To-Be-When-I-Grow-Up' box! It doesn't have to be anything really big though. It can just be something fairly small. It also doesn't have to be kind things that people have done for you. It can be kind things that you have done for other people. That's cool too.

So, grab yourself a big piece of paper, and, yes, you've guessed it…some coloured pens! Woohoo!! And follow the instructions:

1. Draw seven big clouds on the paper in different colours;
2. In three of the clouds, write down three kind things that people have done for you. It can be anything – but they have to be things that have felt really special to you;
3. In three of the clouds, write down three kind things that you have done for other people;
4. In the last cloud, make a Kindness Plan! So, this is something kind that you want to do, but you haven't yet done. Really think about who you would like to do something kind for and what that person might really like;
5. Carry out your Kindness Plan!

So, how did this activity make you feel? It's a good one, I think.

Lots of love,
Lucy
xoxo

Activity 7: Fire Drill

Nee-Nah-Nee-Nah-Nee-Nah!!!

Do you hear the fire engine?? Quick, go and get your fireman's outfit!!!

That is actually a clue for your next activity. I don't really want you to go and get dressed up as a fireman! Ha!

Anyway, no one told me that when I was leaving Mum and Dad's house to go and live with Aunt Lily, Grandma Roberts hid her fire drill idea in one of my bags. Sneaky!

What's a fire drill, I hear you ask. I cannot wait to tell you about this one! It's the most fun thing to create, ever…and really useful too! It really helped the grownups and me when I was upset and when I wasn't doing good listening.

Let me think how Dad explained it to me…

Oh yeah, that was it. So, you know how you practice a fire drill just in case there is actually a real fire, like at your school? It's so you can learn what you and others need to do. So, if there is a real fire (hopefully not!), you've already practiced what to do and you can just get on and do it.

Dad was also telling me how rubbish it would be if you didn't have a fire drill in the first place! He said if the building was on fire then, it would be too late and you might panic and just spend ages trying to get away from the fire, but not really knowing how. Yikes! That does not sound good, does it!?

Anyway, we're not talking about real fires here. We're talking about Feeling-Fires that happen in your head and body – you know, when you're really upset or cross and it feels like your head and body are just bubbling away, ready to explode, like a volcano. Dad said we all have these Feeling-Fires inside of us. He said that sometimes they are just tiny like a candle flame but sometimes they can be as big as the biggest bonfire ever!

So, I use my fire drill when I can feel one of these Feeling-Fires start to burn inside me. It's so I, and everybody around me has a plan. Mr McG knows my fire drill so he can help me. It's so good to have because sometimes when I am really angry, I can't even find my words and that makes me even angrier.

OK. Here we go:

1. Decorate a piece of paper so it looks super cool;
2. Write your name at the top;
3. Write down what your fire drill is. It's OK to get your mum, dad or another grown-up to help you with this;
4. Sit down with your mum and dad, or whoever looks after you and tell them what your fire drill is;
5. Put your fire drill up in the kitchen or another room where it can be seen really easily;
6. Then, whenever you feel your Feeling-Fire starting to burn out of control, tell your family (or another grown-up), then follow your fire drill. Then you can all work together to stop the fire getting big and put it out.

Here's an important rule though. If Mr McG sticks to the fire drill, I have to as well. It's important that I follow my own rules when I am upset, otherwise it doesn't work.

If you're a bit stuck with this activity, here are some things on my fire drill:

- I set a timer for 3 minutes. In that 3 minutes I like to go and be on my own with my animals. It helps me to calm down;
- After the 3 minutes, I always need a big hug;
- After that, I have to go into the kitchen;
- Then I have to talk about what happened with Mr McG.

Do you get how it works? Yeah, course you do! I bet you can come up with some really cool things as well, so let's go and make your fire drill!

Back over to you, Lucy!

Love,
Sarah x

Activity 8: Judgement Day

Hi everybody. It's Lucy again. Now, this activity might not seem like so much fun to you. And I kind of agree. But, keep reading and hopefully you'll see why I decided to put this one in.

Do you remember when I first got that Friends Request from Molly? I went searching through her profile and got so upset and angry when I saw all those happy pictures of her with her mum and dad. Obviously, it was a really tough time for me then, so that kind of explains my reaction.

But, the main point I want to make is that I totally jumped to conclusions when I saw those pictures, didn't I? I mean, I just created this whole idea in my head about Molly – I convinced myself that she was in a happy family and that she was just rubbing it in my face. It's really hard for me to admit all this because I'm actually quite embarrassed by it. I totally judged the whole situation before I had all the facts – I basically decided for myself that I knew what the truth was about somebody else before I knew what the actual truth was. Yikes! That was so not cool of me!

It makes me feel a bit sick when I think that I could have totally missed out on my amazing friendship with Molly if I had decided to stick with what I thought, and not answered her phone-call that day and actually listened to what she had to say.

So, here is your activity:

1. Grab some paper if you want to write this one down (especially if you want to do this one in private). Or, grab somebody that you really trust – somebody that you can talk to about all those serious thoughts in your head. It might not seem like it, but this is actually a really good activity to do with a grown-up who you really like/love;

2. Either write about or talk about a situation or person that made you really sad, angry, upset or frustrated, before you knew all the facts about this situation/person;
3. Write down or tell the person you're with what you thought the truth was in the beginning;
4. Write down or talk about what the actual truth was, once you had learnt it;
5. Write down or talk about whether or not you made a new decision once you had learnt the truth.

Sometimes, it's really hard admitting that you got something wrong or that you judged a situation before you knew the truth (like I did with Molly). But, here's the thing – you will always get things wrong – it's just part of life, part of being a normal human being and kind of how we learn to do things differently. And here's an even better piece of news – grown-ups get it wrong all the time too!

So, don't worry too much about that. The important thing is that maybe you try to be really honest with yourself about stuff like this and to do things a little bit differently next time.

So, I hope you can see why we put this activity in. We just don't want you to miss out on super-cool friendships. Get it?

Lots of love,
Lucy
xoxo

Activity 9: Weekly Routine

Oooo! Yay!!! My turn again!

This activity is so cool! And the good news is, there is not so much talking and thinking, but more doing!

Do you remember after I had been at Aunt Lily's for a while, I got my own little set of jobs to do around the farm, with the animals? Well, this was because I wanted to do them and I really wanted to help with the animals. 'Why?' I hear you ask. Well, because it meant that every day I was doing something to get me to my dream of having my own animal, and that made me feel so amazing! When I filled in Lucy's map (with the stepping stones), I wrote down things like, looking after the injured sheep, collecting the eggs, grooming the horse, feeding the dogs…you know, that kind of thing.

OK, here we go:

1. Choose one of your dreams that you want to come true;
2. Get a piece of paper and write Monday, Tuesday, Wednesday, Thursday, Friday, Saturday and Sunday on it;
3. Now, next to each day write something you could do on that day that will help you reach your dream;
4. Stick to it!

So, now mine looks like this. And it's for reaching my new dream of going to a horse-show with Dandelion. No copying though! Ha!

Monday: Tidy my room (to show Mr McG that I can be tidy and look after my things);
Tuesday: Wash-up after dinner to earn my pocket money;
Wednesday: Ride Dandelion;

Thursday: Help Mr McG for one hour in exchange for hay, for Dandelion;
Friday: Go for a riding lesson;
Saturday: Help Aunt Lily with her sheep;
Sunday: Ride Dandelion.

It really surprised me how quickly my dreams started to come true when I did something towards them, every day. This is so cool, because I know now that if I want something really badly, I can take the right action and I can work on getting it! It's like I get to pretend to be the person I am going to be when I grow up! Woohoo!

You have a go and see what you think… and I bet you have as much fun as I do!

Back over to you, Big Sis.

Love,
Sarah x

Activity 10: Mistakes? What Mistakes?

Hi reader.

It's Lucy – my turn again. So, do you remember my activity about judgement – you know that time I judged Molly and decided she was still part of a happy family, before I knew the truth?

Well, this activity is sort of similar, but maybe not quite so embarrassing. Phew!

This activity is a little bit about mistakes (which are definitely OK to make), but it's mainly about fixing mistakes (which can sometimes be the best bit)! I'm going to use my little sis as an example here because she talks about it non-stop! Wow, that girl can talk! I bet you've noticed that already though, right? She just goes on and on and on and on! And she talks at about a million miles an hour too! Sometimes I totally lose track of what she's saying! I have to hide anything breakable when she visits because she just bounces around, all the time! Have you got any friends like that? Don't tell her I said so, but I do secretly like that about her!

Anyway – here I am getting distracted again! So, the mistake that Sarah goes on about is when she took our 'What-I-Want-To-Be-When-I-Grow-Up-Box' with her, to Aunt Lily's. She thinks she was really mean and that she shouldn't have shouted at me and told me that she thought she should have it. I mean, I get it, she was a bit whiny and she didn't really think about it, but that's OK.

I'm getting distracted again! Anyway, my main point is that she chose to fix what she thought was a big mistake. She made me my very own 'What-I-Want-To-Be-When-I-Grow-Up-Box', got some help from a grown-up and managed to post it all the way to Grandma's house! Awesome! I'm not going to lie – I was ridiculously excited when I got it!

So, you will need paper and coloured pens (woohoo!) again for this one. Here goes:

1.   Draw three big stars on your piece of paper;
2.   In the first star, write about a mistake that you think you have made. This can be anything, but it has to be something that YOU think was a mistake – something that you look back on and think, "oops – don't think I should have done that." I'm not talking about getting a maths question wrong at school – not that kind of mistake. But something that you thought made somebody else a bit sad or angry;
3.   In the second star, write about what you did to fix it;
4.   The third star is for your 'Fix It Plan' – so this is to do with a mistake you think you've made but one that you haven't fixed yet. What do you think you could do to fix it? And this doesn't have to be something huge. It can be something small, like saying 'sorry'.

I'm really proud of you for doing this exercise! It's not easy admitting this stuff about yourself. But, like I said before, it's definitely OK to make mistakes. And it's more than OK to fix them.

See you soon.

Lots of love,
Lucy
xoxo

Activity 11: Feel-Good Box

Hey guys! I'm back!

Do you remember when me and Lucy started to feel a little bit OK about living in our new homes and stopped putting black crosses on our calendars?

There were so many new people to meet and so many new things to try. We didn't really want to do everything at first, even though all these people and things could help us become an even cooler, happier Lucy and Sarah. But we eventually started to say "yes" more and more.

Like the time when Lucy got brave and went round to Molly's for tea, and when I helped with the new sheep that Uncle Fergus brought to the farm? We both started to figure out that it was actually OK to do fun stuff and that we didn't need to be sad all the time. One of the best things we learnt though was that being happy and doing lots of laughing didn't mean we were forgetting Mum and Dad.

We both think that it's really cool to have stuff in your life that makes you giggle and smile, and to have things to look forward to. Lucy calls it 'inspiring' – whatever that means!

So, I'm really excited to plan today's activity for you. It's such a cool one. It's called your Feel-Good-Bag and here's how you create it:

1. Get a really great bag! Lucy would probably tell you to get it from a charity shop, but it doesn't really matter. Of course, you can decorate it with stickers or badges or keyrings if you like;
2. Put seven of your favourite feel good songs on a CD, or an iPod/MP3 or write out a You Tube playlist and put it in your bag;
3. Add your seven favourite photographs to the bag;

4. Add seven objects that are linked to an awesome memory. So maybe like a shell from a holiday or a flower or a piece of horsehair;
5. Get seven post-it notes and write about seven different times you were courageous or brave. This can be anything, even if it's something really small. As long as it's something that felt a bit scary to you but you did it anyway;
6. Add whatever else you want to your Feel Good Bag.

Tada!!! There you have it! Now, when you are feeling sad and need something to make you smile, or there is something you're afraid to do, you can go to your Feel-Good-Bag and remind yourself of what an amazing, incredible, outstanding, super cool person you are.

And the best bit is that you can keep adding to your Feel-Good-Bag whenever you want! There are no rules with this one!

Zoom! Back to you, Luce!

Love,
Sarah x

Activity 12: Let's Get Outside!

Hey everybody!

OK, so this activity is all about getting outside! Hang on a minute, do I sound like a grown-up right now? Are adults around you always telling you to 'turn that T.V off,' or 'put down that phone and get out for some fresh air'! And do they always start those kind of discussions with, "when I was young..."? Haha! Well, it's definitely one of Grandma Roberts's favourite things to talk about! I'm sure she doesn't actually believe that my eyes will turn square 'if I stare at that screen any longer'. Or, does she?

Anyway, I'm getting distracted again. What a surprise! So, you've probably gathered by now that this activity is actually all about getting outside. And once you get into it, it really is pretty cool. If you're anything like Sarah, I bet a person would only have to whisper the word 'outside' and you'd already be at the door with your wellies on! But, if you're anything like me, a lot of what you love to do is probably inside. So, I have come up with a load of different activities that you can do outside...all you need to do is pick the one that looks the most fun to you. You can do them alone or with friends/family/other grown-ups – it's up to you. You will probably have to go with an adult, but they don't have to join in if you don't want them to. Can I let you into a little secret? I seriously do design some of my best clothes when I have been out for some fresh air! Hmmm...maybe grown-ups do sometimes know what they're talking about!

OK...here goes!

Idea 1

You might like to choose this activity if you're one of those people who loves getting an A grade in school or winning a gold medal – losing is not an option! I bet other people tell you that you're always happy and confident too. And, can I ask a personal question? Do you like to spend just that little bit of extra time in front of the mirror to make sure you look goooooood!?

Activity: A Treasure Hunt (but not your ordinary kind of treasure hunt)! Here's what you need to do:

1. Choose something that you're really interested in, like trees, animals, cars, street art, colours, fashion, flowers, buildings (anything you like);
2. Design a really cool chart to take with you on your treasure hunt so you can write down what you see and discover. Don't just hunt for things you know about and see all the time though – hunt for new stuff, and things you've never seen before – set yourself targets for the number of things you're going to find and how quickly you're going to find them, and then try and beat those targets;
3. All that's left is to get out there and do your treasure hunt! Golden rule though – they have to be things you can find outside! No cheating!

When I do this one with Molly, we like to head into town to look for new design and fashion ideas on all the people walking around. I think Sarah likes to go out and look for different birds that she's never seen before.

Idea 2

Are you really curious? And do you always want to understand what's going on and how things work? But, are you quite a shy person and do you prefer to spend more time by yourself? I bet you look at others and think that they're really different to you. That's OK – I do that too, but I'm learning to love the fact that I'm not like everybody else. If I'm sitting on a train platform and a high-speed train goes by, I have to look away and put my fingers in my ears. Grandma Roberts says it's because I'm sensitive, so sometimes things can feel a bit loud or a bit crowded. Do you feel that too? Sorry – I'm getting distracted again – what did I tell you?! Anyway, if you're reading this and thinking, 'hey, that's me', you might just like this activity.

Activity: Curious Cat: Here's what you need to do:

1. Choose something that you're REALLY interested in – it can be cars, buildings, the sky/sun/clouds, trees/flowers, animals, aeroplanes, kite-flying – it doesn't matter but it has to be something you can see outside (now, how did you know I was going to say that?!);
2. Next, get outdoors and study your chosen thing! Watch it, listen to it and remember it. Why do car wheels look like they're spinning backwards when the car is slowing down? How do you know how old a tree is? Why don't aeroplanes fall out of the sky? When you are studying your subject, think of as many questions as you can and have a go at guessing the answers.

Then, when you get home, do some research – how many questions did you get right? And how much new information did you learn? I love this activity! I always end up knowing so much more than when I started! Enjoy!

Idea 3

Are you a person who likes everything to be nice and peaceful? Are you kind and do you love nature? If somebody asks you what you want to do, are you usually pretty happy to just go along with what everybody else is doing? You probably don't like the spotlight and would rather be just a little bit in the background?

Activity: Nature Walk. This is just a nice, simple idea but I love it and I hope you will too!

1. Your walk can be in a wood, in a forest, in a park, or by the coast – it doesn't matter;
2. As you walk around, have a look at all the animals and plants, have a look at the shapes of the clouds in the sky,

listen to the birds, what's the weather like – is it sunny or rainy – what does it feel like on your face? Can you see people walking their dogs? Which is your favourite? If you could be an animal, which one would it be? What would it be like to fly?

There aren't many 'rules' for this activity. This is your walk – you can go fast or slow, a long way or a short way. You can talk or not talk. Play music, or not. Just be you.

Idea 4

You may choose this one if you like things to be perfect, you enjoy figuring things out and you have a really good idea of what you think is right and wrong. For example, you may feel sad if you see certain adverts on TV or you may feel angry if you see somebody dropping litter.

Activity: Outdoor Charity Walk: Here's what you need to do:

1. Choose a charity that means something to you. You may want to donate to an animal charity or a charity for old people – it doesn't matter at all;
2. Find out how to donate to this charity – you may need to ask a grown-up to help you with this;
3. Plan where you are going to do your charity walk – it could be a park, a forest, a town, a beach – the place you live will help you decide. You will also need to work out how long you are going to walk for – you can figure this out in distance or time – so, for example, you may decide you are going to walk for 2 miles or 2 hours;
4. Write a list of who you are going to ask to sponsor you. This could be family, neighbours, friend's parents and/or teachers. It does not matter how many people you have on your list – it's completely OK if it's just one, and it's completely OK if you find five people;
5. Design a sponsorship form – you can do this on the computer or draw it by hand – but you will need to put a title at the top which tells people what kind of charity

walk it is. You will then need to draw a table with 3 columns – one will be for the person's name, one will be for how much they are going to sponsor you for and one will be for their signature. The number of rows in your table will be the same as the number of people you are going to ask for sponsorship money. Some people like it when they know how much sponsor money to give. So, you could perhaps ask for 50p per hour. That's just an idea though – perhaps ask a grown-up what they think;

6. Do your walk! Make sure you take water and a snack with you. And here's a fun twist if you like…why not do the walk a in fancy dress! This could be especially funny if you're doing it with friends!

If you manage to complete the whole walk, you can now collect your sponsor money and donate it to your charity! Amazing!

Idea 5

I bet you choose this activity if you're a person who likes adventure and fun, and are not afraid of new experiences! Are people always telling you how happy and sociable you are? And, come on, admit it, you kind of like being in the spotlight, don't you? I think that's great! I don't really like being centre-stage but love being around people who do! They're always playing and telling stories, and they're always good at loads of different things!

Activity: Do something new! You may need a grown-up to help you with this, but here's my idea:

1. Go somewhere you've never been or try something you've never tried. But, yep, you guessed it – it has to be outside! Maybe there is a new playground or theme-park or zoo near you. Maybe your grown-up will let you try outdoor rock-climbing or roller-skating! Maybe you could go with your friends! Have a race! Climb a tree! Just make sure it's something new to you!

Wow, I wish I could find out what you've decided to do! I bet it's something really fun!

Idea 6

You may choose this one if you like helping people and giving them advice, you work hard in school and you like to be around your friends and other people.

Activity: Gardening: here's what you need to do:

1. Sit down with your mum or dad, or other grown-up and plan an activity that you can do in the garden. This could be to plant something, tidy a flower bed up, clean the bird bath or water the flowers – whatever you like. They may already have a list of things they would like you to do, or perhaps you can come up with some ideas yourself. It's definitely OK to do more than one thing too;

2. I was chatting with Sarah at the weekend and she was telling me about this really cool thing that she and Brody have been working on. They have built an insect hotel! I wasn't sure what she was talking about but she said it's a place for insects to live and that you can easily find instructions on the internet. So, I couldn't wait to tell you about it. She said their next project is to build a hedgehog house! That girl!

Start your activity! Have lots of fun with this one and Sarah said to make sure you get nice and muddy!

Idea 7

OK, so you might choose this activity if you like being the leader and have lots of energy! I bet you love new experiences too and that you're a really good friend to have – you know, I bet you're always sticking up for your besties. Do grown-ups sometimes tell you you're a little bit too honest sometimes though, and that you shouldn't tell people exactly what you think, all the time? Haha!!!

Activity: Obstacle Course! Here it is:

1. Build an obstacle course either in your garden or maybe think of a really new, cool way to get around your local playground or park – maybe it could be your mission to get from the slide to the swings without touching the ground with your feet, or in a record number of minutes? Maybe you could invent a new dance to get around or have different things you need to do when you get to each 'station';
2. Could you maybe use that old piece of wood that your dad has been keeping in the garage, for the course in your garden? Do you maybe want to ask your friends to come and join in so they can share their ideas too – it's totally OK if you want to do it alone though. Can you do the course backwards? Can you do it blindfold?

There's only one rule with this one – HAVE FUN!!!

Idea 8

Are people always telling you that you've got an amazing imagination and that you're always day-dreaming? Are you always making up really creative stories? Do you love beautiful things and the mysterious side of life? If you have said 'yes' to all or most of these questions, you will probably choose this activity!

Activity: Mystery Forest Walk. Here's what you need to do:

1. Visit a woodland or forest near your home. If you haven't got one near where you live, ask your mum, dad or other grown-up if you can plan a trip to one. You might need to do some research to find where there is a really good one;
2. When you get there, walk around, look at everything – the trees, the animals, the pathways…everything!
3. What can you see? Big fallen trees with dark holes in the trunks? Who lives there? Is it an animal, or perhaps a fairy or a unicorn? What do they look like? Do they

have any friends? Who are they? Look up into the tallest trees…who lives there? What used to happen in the forest way before you were born? Was it a forest of dragons and knights, or dinosaurs? How did people used to dress?

When you get home, write a really cool story about a forest creature or a person who used to live in the forest, or maybe you can think of your own ideas…have fun!

Idea 9

You might choose this activity if you're a person who questions everything! Are grown-ups always commenting on the number of questions you ask?! You also like to feel safe and sure about things. Haha – this is so not Sarah – she's so brave – she would fly through the sky on Dandelion if she could – probably without a saddle too! Sometimes you don't really like new places or being around new people, until you get to know them. I bet you're really funny though and that people like to be around you!

Activity: Create something new with something old. Here's what might be fun:

1. Take a favourite toy or activity or play-thing, and think of a new game to play with it. So, if you love playing football, invent a new ball game with it. If you love outside picnics, make something new to eat. If you love going to the park, think of new ways to use the slide or the swings. If you love your bike, try to learn a new trick (with your helmet on though, of course!). If you love taking photos, take pictures of something you wouldn't normally take pictures of. You get the idea;
2. But (and you know what I'm going to say!) – it has to be outside.

Molly is really good at this one! I suggested the picnic idea because this is so her thing! Every time we have a picnic together, she has always thought of something new we can eat or a new drink to try. Being her friend definitely has its advantages!

Idea 10

I just wanted to put one last idea in for those of you who already have lots and lots of ideas in your head, and want to design your own outdoor activity. And, I'm OK admitting that you might have read all my ideas and not liked any of them – well, almost OK admitting it. ;-)

So, my final idea is basically your idea!! Go for it!

Have fun everybody!

Lots of love,
Lucy
xoxo

Activity 13: Animal Omens

"Tweet tweet, tweet tweet," sang the blackbird. Hi. It's me again – Sarah.

I think you know now, how much I love animals! Can I tell you a secret? OK, sometimes I think they are way more fun than people. One of my favourite things to do is go outside and see how many different animals I can spot! It doesn't matter what they are – it could be a bird, a four-legged animal or an insect! I just think they're all so cool!

So, this activity is basically an animal treasure hunt!!! I want you to see how many different types of animal you can find. But wait a minute – that sounds way too easy! Here is an extra fun part…you are going to give each animal a meaning. If you're not quite sure what I'm on about, here is my and Lucy's animal treasure list so far:

When we see a:

Mole: we usually find out something new about ourselves.

Owl: this means that the dream we have dreamed is coming true! But we know we still have to be brave, and keep dreaming and that we have to stay focused on our dream and have no fear!

Wasp: we try to be really enthusiastic and determined with all our activities that day.

Butterfly: this means we try to make a change that day and do something really big and important! It's really fun to wear brightly coloured clothes on these days too!

Blackbird: Haha! I love blackbird days! This is when we listen to music and dance around, and not care or worry what other people think we look like!

Robin: On robin-days we plan a new dream, but we know we have to wait patiently for it to come true! That's the hard part! Ha!

Squirrel: I like squirrel-days too! We always give away something that we no longer need, which makes space for something new to arrive, and helps somebody else make their dream come true! Cool, right?

So, can you think of any other animals and what they could mean? Ooooo…what about a bumble bee or a horse or a dog? Oh my, this is so exciting! Phew, take a breath Sarah!

I so cannot wait to hear what you have come up with!! Quick! Go and get your wellies on and let's go on an animal treasure hunt! I've already got my purple spotty ones on!

Love,
Sarah, x

Activity 14: Seven Areas of Life

Hello readers, it's me, Lucy again. So, hands up if you've ever felt unhappy or a bit bored or like something just isn't quite right? Just so you know, I've got my hand up right now. Yeah, it's not very nice is it? Sometimes, there's a really good reason why you're not feeling so great – like, you didn't do so well in a test at school, or you've fallen out with your best friend or your dad shouted at you, or it's raining outside and you can't think of anything fun to do…whatever the reason, it's so not cool to feel sad.

Well, obviously I can't come up with an activity to cover all the reasons you might be feeling a bit down. Wow! That would be a huge book! Haha! But, I have learnt something pretty cool recently and I can't wait to share it with you. It's kind of based on something Ruth was telling Molly and me about. Do you remember when I'd gone round with my 'What-I-Want-To-Be-When-I-Grow-Up' box that Sarah had sent to me? And do you remember that Ruth was telling us about all the different areas in our lives and how it's important to try to do something in each of those areas? That's what my next activity is about.

OK…you know the drill by now…go grab yourself a big piece of paper and some coloured pens (did I tell you how much I LOVE coloured pens?!). And follow the steps:

1. On your piece of paper, draw seven big circles or clouds or squares…whatever you want…make them different colours though so it looks really cool;
2. At the top of each of your shapes write out the following headings: SCHOOL, YOURSELF, FAMILY, FRIENDS, CHORES/MONEY, HOBBIES, DREAMS;
3. Underneath each of the headings, write down what you like to do in each of these areas.

If you're a bit stuck, here's what mine looks like: SCHOOL: I really like art and French; YOURSELF: I really like to spend time on my own, just listening to music or looking at some fashion magazines. If the weather is nice, I like doing this in the garden; FAMILY: I like spending time with Grandma Roberts and cooking for her; FRIENDS: Hanging out with Molly or my new school friends; CHORES/MONEY: Molly and I clean Ruth's car every week and help her with her food shopping. We get some pocket money for doing this; HOBBIES: Well, I think you know by now that my main hobby is clothes design, but I have also joined a gymnastics group at school, which I LOVE! DREAMS: My big dream is still to be a fashion designer!

Now, here's the cool part. If I am having one of those days when I am feeling a bit down or a bit bored or just not quite right, I go straight to my Seven Areas Chart and do a bit of detective work! I can pretty much guarantee that I will discover where the problem is! It will either be that one of the areas isn't going so well, which I then fix. If it's not that, it's usually because I have been doing too much in one of the areas and not really focusing on the others. This usually makes me sad because I actually miss doing all the other stuff when I don't do it.

So, have a go with this. Honestly, it's such a cool activity to do!

Lots of love,
Lucy
xoxo

Activity 15: Money, Money, Money

Hey everyone,

Guess whose back? Sarah's back!

So, let's roll onto our next activity! This is definitely one you can get your guardians or family to join in with. I know some people may say you're too young, but trust me, if you can get good at this, life suddenly becomes so much more fun! You may notice, like I do, that everyone always seems to be talking about or arguing over this. Have you worked out what I'm talking about yet? Well, Mr McG did this activity with Brody and then Brody helped me set it up too. Now it's my turn to share it with you. Woohoo!

Have you guessed what I'm going on about yet? Nope?

Oh boy!

OK, let me spell it out: it's M-O-N-E-Y.

My dad always used to say this one thing to me…learn to manage your money or your money will manage you. I don't quite understand what he was talking about though. Maybe you could explain it for me, or ask a grown-up. But then my dad was always coming out with some weird stuff!

Anyway, I love, love, love doing this activity, and I do it every week! Here's what you need to do:

1. Get four clear, glass jars. There may be some spare ones in the cupboards at home or you could probably find some in a charity shop. They don't need to match though – you could even get ones in different colours! Oh, but make sure you ask first before you go hunting in cupboards. I made that mistake – oops;

2. Get some sticky labels;

3. Grab some coloured pens (Lucy would love that bit!) and write DREAM on one label, PLAY on another,

LEARNING on the third one and GIVING on the last one;

4. Stick one label onto each jar. You should now have a DREAM jar, a PLAY jar, a LEARNING jar and a GIVING jar;

5. Next, ask your parents (or whichever big people you live with) for some 1ps, 2ps, 5ps and 10ps. These are just to practice with though until you get your own money. Don't forget to give it back to them!

6. Put 25% of what you receive in each jar. Mr McG taught me that 25% is a quarter but I still needed a bit of help dividing up my money.

It's totally not as tricky as you think. I mean, if Brody can do it, then I definitely know you can do it too! Maybe when you start to get your own money, your grown-ups can help you, just until you get the hang of it. But, it will look something like this:

If you receive £1, you then put 25p in your DREAM jar, 25p in your PLAY jar, 25p in your LEARNING jar and 25p in your GIVING jar.

If you receive £2, you then put 50p in your DREAM jar, 50p in your PLAY jar, 50p in your LEARNING jar and 50p in your GIVING jar.

See how it works?

What do the jars mean, I hear you ask! Well, your DREAM jar is to help you save any money that's needed to reach one of your dreams, like go and visit a place or buy something special. Your PLAY jar is for when you need some money to go out with your friends and want to buy an ice cream or something. Your LEARNING jar is for buying books, or maybe visiting a really cool museum. Your GIVING jar is so that you can buy things for other people, like buying your brother or sister, or friend a birthday present.

Are you wondering where to get the money from? Well, some of you will get pocket money, so you can put that in your jars. I don't get pocket money, but I do get money from Mr McG and Aunt Lily for helping around their houses and on the farms. Hey, you could sell something that you made. Lucy made a really cool purse and Grandma Roberts bought it off her. Have a think, either on your own or with your grown-ups, and I bet you can come up with some really cool ideas!

It is so cool to see the jars fill up and then, when I want to get something, I can! And if I haven't got enough, then I just wait until I do.

Back over to you Lucy!

Love,
Sarah, x

Activity 16: Pay It Forward

Well, hello again! It's Lucy! I'm so glad you're still here and I really hope you're enjoying all our activities! It has been so much fun for us too!

So, my next activity is a really cool one! Haha – I say that about them all, don't I?

OK – do you remember when Molly and I headed down to the charity shops in town to pick up some clothes and accessories for Lolly Label? Oh yeah, that's when Molly was teasing me about my big feet – cheeky! Anyway, how amazing that we were able to use clothes that somebody else didn't want to help make our dreams come true!

OK, so your next activity goes like this:

1. Find a big, rubbish bag or carrier bag;
2. Go into your room and have a look to see if there is anything in there that you don't use/wear/need/want;
3. Put the things in the bag;
4. Go through the bag with your mum, dad or whoever you live with, just to make sure they are happy for you to get rid of the things that are in there;
5. Plan a trip to a charity shop;
6. Take your bag to the charity shop and DONATE! ☺

I would love to know what you donated to the shop! I really do love this activity and I really love thinking about somebody walking into the shop and finding an old treasure of mine and it becoming a new treasure of theirs!

Happy donating everybody!

Lots of love,
Lucy
xoxo

Activity 17: Selfie Video

Five, Four, Three, Two, One! Blast off!!!

Hi guys! It's Sarah again! Do you remember when Mr McG got me to stand in front of the mirror and he said to me, "The girl you see in the mirror is the girl you are going to be," or something like that anyway. Sometimes I don't always get what he's on about! Ha!

Well, I did actually listen to him this time and, don't tell him I said this, but he was kind of right! Ever since I started to look at myself differently, I began to act differently and even talk differently – I even use new words now that Lucy would be proud of. I just looked in the mirror one day and thought, *'yup, I'm a proper horse rider and I have loads of my own animals.'* It's pretty cool! Nope, actually it's flippin' amazing!

OK, so are you ready? Of course you are! Just before we get started though, if you're a boy-reader, make sure you don't say, 'girl'! Ha!

Woah! Hang on a minute! We're not going to use mirrors. We are going to do this Cool-Kid-Style! Let's go!!! Time to make your New Me Video!!!

1. Take out your phone if you have one, or ask a grown-up if you can borrow theirs;
2. Turn the camera setting onto video;
3. Grab a piece of paper and write down seven things you want to see more of in yourself. But you have to say it like it's already true. For example: 'I have won a medal for gymnastics', 'I have really good friends at school', 'I am the world's best footballer'. You get the idea;
4. Then either get a selfie stick or one of your friends to record you;
5. Read your list of seven things out loud into the camera, and repeat three times;

6. Then every morning or night, watch the video once, that's it.

Ground rule! When you are talking into the camera you have to look directly into it so that when you watch it back, you are looking straight at yourself – and can see the amazing person that you are!

You can do this as many times as you like. You may need to change your video a bit or come up with new sayings as you go along, but you get the idea. And if you are anything like Lucy, you will always be watching videos on YouTube or Facebook! It's just that now, you are spending time watching a video all about you and your dreams! Cool!

Tally-ho! Your turn Lucy!

Love,
Sarah x

Activity 18: Letter from the Future

Hi reader.

Awww – this is my last activity. It's really sad but it's also really exciting because it means that you have almost made it to the very last one! Yup, don't worry – there is one more, but Sarah and I will be doing that one together. Haha – yeah, I know – Sarah and I doing something together! Yikes! Let's see if Sarah will actually give me chance to speak! Probably not – she will probably just go on and on and on and on again, and bounce around and be all 'Sarah'! Gosh, I hope she has a wash first. I am so NOT working on anything with her if she stinks of sheep poo! Ewwwww!

Oh, look at me getting all distracted again! So, I've put this activity near the end because hopefully you will be able to put everything you have learnt so far into it. And, secretly, it's probably my favourite! So, you know how we have been talking about making dreams come true and working towards becoming the person you really want to be when you are a grown-up? Well, in this activity you get to pretend you are that grown-up and that all of those dreams HAVE come true! It's so cool! Let me explain. You are going to write a letter to…YOU! Yes, that's right – the pretend grown-up you is going to write a letter to the real you now!

Let's get started! I can't wait anymore! Here's what to do:

1. Grab a pen and some pieces of paper;
2. Write your own name and the age you are now at the top of the page;
3. Start your letter! Include things like what you did to make your dreams come true; was it easy or was it difficult; did you make any mistakes and if so, how did you fix them, what have you learnt, how you feel now

that your dreams have come true. It's basically a chance for the grown-up you to teach the younger you what you learnt!

4. Use your imagination and make your letter as funny and crazy and clever and silly and serious as you like! It can be long or short, private or not. It's your letter – have fun with it!

In my letter, I pretended that I was a proper, grown-up fashion designer with Molly, and that Lolly Label clothes were being sold in actual shops and could be seen in magazines and everything! I told the younger me not to give up and that even the small things Molly and I did all counted! I also told the younger me not to bother trying too hard to match the yellow shoes with the little green flowers to anything! Ha! That really did not work!

OK…so there we go! That's it.

I can't say goodbye to you – it's too sad. I feel like I know you! So I will just say, 'see you soon'! I have a sneaky feeling I will! ;-)

Lots of love,
Lucy
xoxo

Activity 19: New You – New Environment

Hi guys! So, here we are together! This is pretty much how it has started:

Sarah: *"Yes, Lucy, I have had a shower this week!"*

Lucy: *"Are you sure? You still smell a bit animal-pooey to me!"*

Sarah: *"Take that!"*

Lucy: *"Ouch! No pinching, Sarah!"*

Sarah: *"Well, be nice then, big sis!"*

Hmmm…what do you reckon our chances are for getting to the end of this activity!? But, we promised you, readers, so here we are together to give it our best shot! Haha!

Sarah: *"Yep! And this is probably my most favourite one yet!"*

Lucy: *"Sarah! They are all your favourite ones."*

Sarah: *"OK then, smarty-pants, why don't you tell our amazing readers what they need to do."*

Lucy: *"Don't worry, I will. Ouch! Quit pinching me, Sarah!"*

Oh dear! ;-)

So, this activity is all about changing your bedroom to match the new you! You might be wondering why changing your bedroom is important, and what that has to do with becoming a new person. Well, it's simple – you can't do a very good job of being the new you if your bedroom matches the old you. Changing your bedroom can help you to dream bigger! It becomes like a space in which you can pretend to be the person you want to be when you grow up. And it can help you to stay focused on your dreams. Are you still with me?

Sarah: *"Oh, yaaaawn! Lucy, can you just let them get on with the activity already!"*

Lucy: *"All right, all right! You do some of the talking then, Sarah!"*

OK, so here's what you need to do:

1) Go into your bedroom and have a good look around, and I mean a good look around – go into your wardrobe, your drawers, have a look on your shelves and on your book case. And if you're really feeling brave, under your bed! I made the mistake of going under Brody's bed once! Yikes! I nearly didn't make it back!

2) Next, put anything that doesn't match the new you, or the person you want to be in the centre of the room;

3) When you've got time and after you've asked a grown-up, you can follow Lucy's Charity Shop activity with all this stuff. Cool, right?

4) Then, make a list of the things you want to bring into your bedroom, and the changes you want to make. I can already feel you getting excited about this!

5) When you're happy with your list, start to bring in the things that you can afford or get hold of now. Or, if you can't quite afford something yet, start to put some of your pocket money to one side so you can start saving;

6) Now, here comes the best bit! Start reorganising your room!

SARAH: When I moved into my new room at Aunt Lily's, she told me I could make some changes to it. So, we went into town and bought a new lamp and a duvet set which had animals on it. I didn't wear my flowery sandals or pink t-shirts anymore, so I took them to the charity shop. This left a bit of space in my wardrobe which I filled with my new wellies and coat. Aunt Lily had a picture of some horses which she didn't want anymore, so I put that up instead of the one that was hanging in my room when I moved in. I also used one of Aunt Lily's spare rugs. I put this next to my bed to keep my toes warm when I got out of bed. And it's green, which is my favourite colour, so my room looked really cool after this. I did the same kind of thing in my new room at Mr McG's too!

135

LUCY: Well, I really wanted a new bookshelf putting up in my room, for my fashion magazines. So, I found a piece of old wood in Grandma's garage and Carl, the postman, put it up for me, which was so kind! We made him a cup of tea that day and gave him some nice biscuits to say thank you! Then, I made my own curtains out of some material I bought from a charity shop. I also went through my wardrobe and realised that I wasn't really wearing black anymore, so I took those clothes to the charity shop. This made room in my wardrobe for all my new colourful clothes. I really love purple and blue now!

We both think you're going to love doing this activity! We absolutely love our new rooms, and we think that they really suit the new us. We really like waking up in the morning and seeing all this stuff that we have collected and wearing these clothes that suit who we have become and who we want to be.

So, put this book down and let's get cracking!

Lots of love,
Lucy and Sarah
xoxo

Activity 20: Secret Activity

We may just have told a little fib there. Activity 19 wasn't really the last one. We have one more for you but it is actually your parents/adults who have been given all the instructions, so feel free to go and ask them all about it.

Conclusion

One final thing…

We are so proud of all of you, for the journey that you have taken with us. Try to think back to who you were when you started this book. Do you feel different now? How has your life changed? What was your favourite activity? We'd love to know!

We hope that this journey and all these activities have shown you that you can use all your new skills and ideas all the time, whenever you want – even when you are a grown-up.

We are going to miss you loads and loads, but somehow, we know this is not the end. In fact, it is just the beginning.

Lots of Love,
Lucy and Sarah
xoxo

Part 3
Adult's Guide

Contents

Adult's Guide

So, you're the guardian of a 'Tween'? No, we're not referring to an odd, foam T.V character – we're talking about that strange species of child who lies somewhere between loveable bundle and rebellious teenager. Have you heard of the Terrible Twos? Well, this is the Terrible Tweens! Here are a few things you may have realised: they are too cool for school – you are not. Their friends are cool – you are not. They know exactly what a 'selfie' and a 'vlog' is – you do not. They can do 'The Floss' – you most certainly cannot – well, not without considerable damage to a hip, anyway. They say 'Snapchat', you say 'Snap-what'? You are not cool, remember?

It's not all bad though. They may still want to send their parents a text at bedtime from that long-awaited sleepover. And they may still want to share a secret with you, as long as their friends aren't in ear-shot though, of course. And a lucky few of you may still be allowed a cuddle! And one thing is guaranteed…they will most certainly make your belly laugh and your heart sing.

OK, so Lucy and Sarah have hopefully awakened the dream muscle within your children, and we all know what that means. Your little volcanos are probably going to erupt with a whole bunch of questions, shopping lists, ideas, thoughts and probably a huge request for your time.

Before we start though, this is what we are not…

This is not a child psychology book or a lengthy text book. We are not going to fill your minds with technical words or overwhelm you with theories and statistics. And we certainly aren't going to tell you that this book is the answer to all your problems. There are plenty of amazing books out there already, with that kind of information right at your finger-tips.

We're also not here to tell you how to be a fantastic parent/nanny/guardian/key worker – we already know you've got that covered.

Whether or not you are a biological parent, a foster parent, a Grandad, a support worker or other related professional, we believe that some of the over-riding principles throughout this book can be used effectively, by one and all. Parents will likely want to go through this journey with their own children. Whereas, as mentioned, professionals can use the three-book project directly with the children they are caring for/educating and/or as a teaching resource with the families they are working alongside. We don't mind – we want you to use it in the best way for you.

You will notice certain repeated themes throughout the series. These draw from our own personal experiences of working directly with parents, professionals and children, and from our own lives. You will hear us talk about balance, lack of resistance, motivation, fulfilling dreams and honesty. Bear with us – we are not going to take you on an airy-fairy journey – this is all based on real 'stuff', real life, real emotions and real experiences. But we feel that somewhere in here lies the key to a more fulfilled life. These are the principles that we try to live by, every day. Worth a go, right?

OK, now, this is what we are...

We are two women who have spent over thirty years, between us, guiding and educating parents and children, in very different ways. But we have always infiltrated our life principles into this teaching. We're here to inspire, suggest, motivate and bring hope. We have created this separate section for you because we want to help you guide your enthusiastic munchkins along the journey. But, we're also secretly hoping that you will want to complete some of the activities too. This should give you a deeper understanding of why we have chosen these specific activities and what we believe they can teach us. You never know – you may just discover a few hidden treasures of your own as well.

We have started to notice in our work that parents/carers can sometimes get lost in a world of too much knowledge. Whilst we believe it can be beneficial to live with a wealth of information just a click away, we have found that people can sometimes be left uncertain about what feels 'right' for them and for the children in their care. There are too many opportunities to listen to other people's opinions online, instead of listening to one of the most important opinions out there – yours. So, we have scrapped the technical and gone back to basics. We have created a space for you to discover your own internal guide, be it gut feelings, observations, or wise lessons passed down from previous generations.

Ground Rule for the parents, in particular: (I bet you thought those were just for the children!):

Your role on this journey is to be a guide for and guardian of your children. It is not to be their best friend – they already have one or some of those. They sometimes need somebody to look up to – let that be you. But, in order to be the best guardian you can be, we feel it's important that you make regular pit stops along the road, to re-fuel yourself. After all, you can't drive a car without petrol in it. You need to take time to love, nourish and nurture yourself as well. If you learn how to do this, imagine the message you are passing onto your children – that it's OK to take care of yourself and do things that make YOU feel good.

You may be wondering how on earth you're going to fit these 'pit-stops' in. How about trying to create a small slot of time that becomes known in your household as 'You Time'. It only needs to be half an hour, but the rules are that nobody interrupts you when you are in 'You Time'. If you are consistently firm about the boundaries with this AND your little stars also see you actively create slots of time for both of you to do something together, they are more likely to respect this. By the way, 'You Time' is not for unloading the dishwasher or making dinner, it's for sitting with a cup of tea, calling a friend or exercising – whatever makes you feel more like you.

One Size Does Not Fit All:

Over the years, we have worked with children of many sizes, shapes, colours, backgrounds and characters. Our techniques have been tweaked, modified, celebrated, laughed at and, sometimes, thrown completely out the window. One size most certainly does not fit all. Each child has their own tastes, likes, dislikes, ideas, personality traits, quirks and ambitions. And you know what? Thank goodness!

We always aim to nurture each child's personality and help them to be the best version of themselves that they can be, whatever that looks like. The 'Tween' years are a particularly special time for exploration and self-discovery – there will be a lot of questioning, figuring things out and working out who fits where and why. This is not about who we want them to be or who we think they should be – this is about them.

We would like to encourage you to be observant, hesitant, patient and nurturing. What do your children like to do? Are they outgoing or shy? Messy or organised? Sensitive or not? Careful or brave? None of these traits are right or wrong, good or bad, better or worse – they just are…and that's OK. We firmly feel that each child should be taught that it's OK to be them.

Nothing is fixed though – your children will likely go through all sorts of different phases, and elements of their character will most certainly shift and change – step back, have a look, allow. Their traits will become more 'fixed' in adulthood – but now is a time for learning and development. But, given the 'right' circumstances and experiences, we believe a child can always thrive and succeed.

See if you can recognise any of your children in one or some of the following descriptions:

1) These little treasures like to question everything. They like security and they can be a bit wary of something if they don't feel it's safe. They want people to like them so will try hard to entertain and make others laugh. They might often surprise you with how much they can empathise with what another person is feeling. However, their moods can change and they can become insecure and apprehensive. They may even hide their feelings. **Note to adults:** try to guide them in decision making and support them in new situations as these can sometimes be quite hard for them. They don't like the unknown so try to remain consistent for them. These children will also appreciate a break from trying so hard all the time and worrying about pleasing others. So, try

to ensure they have some alone/'down' time, within which they can just be themselves and have fun;

2) These little munchkins like things to be perfect. They enjoy working things out, especially if it follows a logical pattern. They may have a real sense of what they feel is right and wrong – you may even have witnessed the odd 'tut' and raised eyebrow at dropped litter or cruelty of some kind. They like to be responsible, but they may not be able to express their anger easily and may show awareness that others don't seem to worry like they do. **Note to adults:** encourage lots of fun and creativity, through non-competitive activities;

3) These little jewels love adventure and fun, and they are not afraid of new experiences. They are happy, sociable, self-assured and curious, and they love the spotlight. They like to tell stories and to play, and they can have many talents. They want to be free! **Note to adults:** try not to worry if it seems like they don't commit to anything in particular – they are gaining a lot of knowledge and experience from their many interests and pursuits, and will relish your support. Try to keep things interesting, but be observant about when something has hurt or bothered them;

4) These little dreamers are all about feelings and beauty. They have a vivid imagination and will often engage in make-believe play. They are probably quite arty and creative, and they love mystery, music and films. They can sometimes get sad or bored by normal life though. They can be shy and get overwhelmed by their feelings. They may also have a tendency to loll about and can sometimes be quite clingy. They will sometimes prefer to be 'behind the scenes'. They can be easily hurt though, and stubborn at times. **Note to adults:** really listen to what they're saying about their feelings – you may not relate, but it's real to them. Don't push them into busy, social situations if this makes them uncomfortable – they need alone time. Try to treat them gently. Give them extra time to share their thoughts and wind down;

5) These little gems are sociable, happy and confident. You are likely caring for a high-achiever! They may take an intriguing interest in their own appearance. They are interested in lots of different things and can excel at a number of them. They have agile minds and like to teach and to guide. Failure is not a word in their dictionary! They have lots of energy but can burn out easily. **Note to adults:** try to encourage some down-time, and for them to get in tune with their inner-world, so they are not so concerned with outside appearances. If your children have a bit of a temper, try to be straightforward and honest with them, and keep cool when they are not. Choose your battles;

6) These little detectives are really curious, and want to understand what's going on and how things work. They are probably quite shy and introverted, preferring their own company to that with others. You may have heard them express concerns about feeling different, and they may be sensitive to incoming information, such as loud noises or too-crowded places. **Note to adults:** try not to push social interactions, and try to understand that change and new situations can be difficult for them.

One last thing before we let you get on. Have a think about how your children like to be praised and rewarded. What makes them feel loved and motivated to repeat what they have just done?

- Do they like to be told in words what they have done well, or what you like about them/their behaviour?
- Do they feel proud of visual praise, such as a certificate or trophy?
- Do they love physical contact from you, like hugs and kisses?
- Do they perhaps want to spend some time with you as a reward, either to engage in something they love to do, or just for the pleasure of being in your company?
- Do they express happiness when you have offered to do something for them, such as help them tidy up or fix something that has broken?

- Do they get great enjoyment from you organising a surprise for them?
- Are they motivated by gifts?
- Or, do you perhaps have a child who shies away from too much spotlight and praise?

You may not realise it, but the 'way' you express love/praise to children can be so much more powerful if you give it in a way that each child can easily receive. Try asking them what they prefer – you may be surprised by the answers.

OK, let's get started!

Activity 1: Box of Dreams

This first activity is designed to allow children to explore and ignite their imaginations, rather than being shown a reality through, for example, a computer game or T.V. programme. Try to encourage your children to create this activity using their own minds only, from start to finish. When your children begin to explore the different dreams they have, allow their imaginations to stretch and be outrageous! (There is an activity later on to help them make more concrete plans to enable these dreams to come true). This is a delightful, open-ended activity and does not need to be over-complicated.

It has been created to facilitate the following three concepts:

♥ To allow children to dream and bring that dream into their reality without the Hollywood-drama spin on it.

We are finding more and more that dreams and drama are getting a little too intertwined. We feel that movies, in particular, portray the idea that when a dream comes true it must have glitter and glamour attached to it. We are more interested in real-life dreaming and the reality of what that entails. Don't get us wrong, there is definitely a time and a place to grab the popcorn and escape into magical-movie night. But, we are trying to teach and encourage an understanding of the difference.

♥ To allow children to have their own dreams and not get swayed by what other people are doing and/or wanting.

Children can put an awful lot of pressure on themselves to, for example, follow the interests of their friends or siblings, or try to people-please at home/school. We are therefore concerned with teaching children to feel comfortable exploring their own likes and dislikes, and basing their dreams on these. We want them to stay true to the morals and beliefs they currently have, and not be afraid to incorporate these as they begin to dream. Giving them space to explore their own viewpoints in this way will help them to determine which are theirs and ones they want to keep, and which are not. They may discover new ideas or bring to the surface those that they have been hiding. There are a number of factors which could be affecting your children's willingness to 'speak up', such as self-worth or fear. Your role is to listen to what seems to feel right to your children and support this. Of course, it may all change tomorrow, but that's OK.

♥ To allow children to believe in opportunities and their unlimited potential in life.

This concept may challenge you as well as the children, but that's OK. Life can be challenging – it's what you do with that challenge that makes the difference. This part of the activity focuses on highlighting to children that even the people they see as a hero or a role model had to start somewhere. These 'heroes' are still human beings, like them, and have taken a journey or certain steps to get to where they are today. This is actually good news for you because it means that a path has already been carved. This is all about allowing your children to start to bridge the gap between them and their 'heroes' (their 'heroes' being the people who have perhaps got what they want or are doing something they want to do). We want them to see that reaching your dreams isn't something reserved for a select few, but that they are just as worthy and just as capable. We want them to change the way they see themselves and truly believe that even though the path we take might be different, the same opportunities are available to us all.

You will have noticed Lucy and Sarah encouraging your children to dream big. We'd just like to clarify here that we are not talking about trying to encourage every child to become a rocket scientist. We're talking about all types of dreams, and children being taught how to reach for the dreams that are big to them. And here's the thing – what is a big dream to one child might not be a big dream to another child, but all dreams are just as important as each other. If your child's biggest dream is to have a friend over for dinner, this is just as incredible as another child wanting to be the next Taylor Swift.

Trigger questions:

- ♥   Tell me what makes you really happy;
- ♥   What do you like doing the most?
- ♥   What is your dream?
- ♥   What would you like to put in your What-I-Want-To-Be-When-I-Grow-Up box?

Activity 2: Tribe Dream

This activity is all about dreaming again (you'll get used to this!). It looks at another aspect of dreaming though. We feel it's important for children to understand that it can take many hands to make a dream come true – that there are people behind the scenes, at the side-lines and on centre stage. It's about helping them to acknowledge and appreciate all contributions from all different people when working towards a big, collective dream.

It has been created to facilitate the following three concepts:

♥ To teach children that they might not be good at something their friend excels at, or vice versa – and to understand the value of that.

We feel this is a fairly self-explanatory message – that it is not just OK to be different, it is actually better to be different. We want children to feel proud of their strengths and learn how to voice this without sounding arrogant. Your children will probably be trying extra hard to fit in right now. This may lead them to lean towards people who are like them, for fear of standing out. So, this activity is designed to encourage them to welcome different people with different personality traits into their lives. If your children are struggling to understand this concept, perhaps you'd like to use the example of the Aboriginal Tribes as described in Lucy and Sarah.

♥ To teach children to work as a team or community, but without loss of their identity.

We have been asked many times how on earth it was possible to successfully co-author a book, and how we managed to work together. So, we'd like to share a little of our journey here. We both had initial reservations about how it was going to work, but after a cup of tea and a chat, we soon realised that the reason we were going to work so well as a team was because we have such different strengths.

Sam: I have a slightly obsessive love of editing and making sure commas are in the right place. This is Naomi's worst nightmare!

Naomi: I prefer to openly dream and rapidly tap out stories on the keys. I'm more than happy to leave the 'prettying' to Sam!

We also discovered that our tribe of two was enough at the writing stage of these books. Your children may want lots of people in their tribe or they may, like us, only want a couple. Both are perfect.

♥   To teach children to let go of control and listen. But also to have responsibility for their role in the tribe.

Your children may struggle with having things done in a different way to the way they want them to be done. They may struggle with being a team player. Or, you may experience the other extreme. Your children may just want someone else to make all the decisions and they may not be comfortable contributing or sharing their strengths. This activity is about working with the child in front of you and trying to rebalance the scales a little. We want them to feel confident being themselves, but to also acknowledge the strengths of others and how they might contribute to the big dream.

Your children may well go through the process of criticising others and others criticising them. Don't worry – this is a natural part of exploring who they are, where they fit and who is like them.

If they are criticising others, give them the opportunity to voice their worries without trying to fix it straight away. Let your little volcanoes let off some steam. It's your role to find out why they are criticising another child and, just as importantly, which traits/actions they are criticising. The next step is to help them see that perhaps this is just something that particular child doesn't excel at. The solution is then to ask your children to tell you about the other child's strengths. Give examples of your own and/or other people your child knows. This will help to redirect their focus.

If your children are receiving the criticism, your first job is to just listen to what they are feeling. This may be very upsetting for them. Then, when you're ready, encourage your children to identify which trait/action has been criticised. If it is one of their weaknesses, ask them to tell you what they are good at. Give examples of your own and let them know that it's impossible be good at everything.

Either way, we would like your children's actions/thoughts to be based on love, rather than fear or jealousy of others. Remind your children every day that perfection does not exist so that they can free themselves from any pressure to be so.

Trigger questions:

- ♥ Who do you want to be in your tribe?
- ♥ What is the tribe's big dream?
- ♥ What skills does the tribe need for that dream to come true?
- ♥ Which of the skills do you have?
- ♥ Which of those skills do the other members have?

Activity 3: Being Thankful

Before we get started on this activity, we would just like to say that we are only too aware of how whiney and self-centred a Tween can be! Ha-ha! So, we are under no illusions that this activity is going to turn them into the next Zen Buddha. However, if your children do suddenly start sitting on a mountain-side in a perfect Yoga position, expressing immense gratitude for all that is, we want to know about it!

Joking aside though, we do believe it's important for children to learn to look back over their day with a bit of reflection and balance. We know that sounds a little 'out there', but in simpler terms, we feel children should be able to acknowledge their achievements, their mistakes and also the environment they live in, and the people around them. This will help to build self-awareness and it's also a chance for them to feel different emotions.

As with all our activities, we are hoping to encourage your children to focus on their own experiences and feelings, not what they think they should think or feel. We want this to be a safe space for them to freely express themselves without fear of being laughed at or steered in any way.

It has been created to facilitate the following three concepts:

♥   To teach children to look back on their day in a balanced way and not just focus on the negative.

Let's be realistic here…we are a world of whingers and we love to look back on our day and think about all the things that went wrong! Ha-ha! So, this activity has been created to encourage your children to also think about the things that went well, and the things that made them smile. What's nicer than that?

♥ To steer children away from taking things for granted and teach greater appreciation for the people/experiences around them.

It could be very easy for your children to over-look, for example, being invited to a friend's house for dinner, being given a gift or winning a game. It could also be very easy for them to assume that this is how life is and should be. This, of course, wouldn't be their fault, but there is a big difference between feeling entitled and feeling grateful. We are obviously interested in the latter. As mentioned, we are not expecting endless, soppy words of gratitude. We are simply trying to raise awareness and acknowledgement that it is a privilege to receive.

♥ To teach children to listen, talk about and reflect on their day.

We feel it's more than OK to help children learn that, at times, they may need to listen to others, hear their points of view, discuss how that makes them feel but also to take a moment to appreciate what the last 24 hours has included. We all know that, as you grow older, it no longer feels like the hours flying by, but the years. If your children develop the skill of appreciating a single day, it's more likely to be remembered.

It is also just nice to sit for a moment and talk.

Trigger questions:

♥ What did you enjoy today?
♥ What made you smile today?
♥ Is there anything that makes you feel really good inside?

Activity 4: Your Dream

Cast your minds back to Activity 1 for a second. We encouraged you to encourage your little ones to dream big! This activity is all about turning those big dreams into reality, and researching the steps that may be involved. Your role here is to simply guide. It's not our job to rush in and tell a child that their dream is unachievable – we would like them to figure out by themselves what it might take to achieve their dream, and whether or not they are willing to try. Your responsibility here is to perhaps help them find the information they need in order to make that decision. Some of the steps and ideas they come up with are going to be unrealistic (that's just the way a Tween mind works)! But, this is where you can step in to gently help them determine what is realistic and what is not.

Be aware that at some points in this activity, your guidance may be affected by your own beliefs and what you feel is achievable. We know it's hard to put yourself aside in situations like these, but try to be receptive, keep your mind open and let you little soldiers try.

This activity will also help your children learn how to plan a sequence of actions and events that may need to occur to get them to their dream – a bit like stepping stones. Your role is to ensure that the sequence runs in a logical order. This will also help them to stay focused on their present stepping stone, and not try to skip ahead.

It has been created to facilitate the following three concepts:

♥ To help teach children the difference between a wish and a dream.

When you are having a chat with your little ones about this, remind them of the conversation Mr McGever had with Sarah about this very topic. He defined a wish as making a statement but taking no action. And he defined a dream as making a statement and coming up with a plan to make it come true.

This activity will therefore help your children to be proactive, learn how to make decisions and how to take action towards a goal.

♥ To help teach children how to formulate a realistic plan.

This is where your children may go a little 'off-piste' with their ideas, but that's OK. We're more concerned with them having the freedom to use their imaginations to their fullest, and to continue to develop their skill of formulating a plan. At this point, the result is almost irrelevant. It's more about them just giving it a go. As mentioned though, your responsibility is to help them decipher which steps are achievable and which aren't. For example, if their dream is to be in a national gymnastics competition, clearly, this can't be step one of the plan. A training schedule needs to be put in place that they can work on each day or each week. This may include something as simple as the provision of a foam mat for them to practice forward rolls at home, and/or being signed up to join a gymnastics club. This will also help you to monitor commitment and expenditure, particularly in the early stages, when a dream may reveal itself to simply be a short-lived curiosity. Either way, each step should be achievable, but still challenging. This will help to create a sense of achievement and success along the way. If you set unachievable goals, you are more likely to become discouraged and give up.

♥ To teach children how to take responsibility for their dream coming true.

We have started to see an increase in armchair dreaming! This is when a person lives with a 'wish mind-set'. They may state clearly which dream they would like to come true, but will then sit in their armchair simply waiting for that to happen.

A person going into the Olympics didn't just turn up on race day and win a medal. They had to prepare – physically, mentally and emotionally, and train to become that person. Although there would have been a team of helpers every step of the way, nobody else could have taken that journey for them. It also isn't something they could have achieved without action. We would like your children to truly grasp the concept that action is necessary for dreams to come true. We would like them to embrace the work that may be involved, and to face the setbacks as well as the successes.

Trigger questions:

- ♥ What is your big dream?
- ♥ What do you need to do to get there?
- ♥ Do you think you can do that?
- ♥ Do you need anything for it?
- ♥ How can I help?
- ♥ What are the 7 actions you are going to take?

Activity 5: Feelings' Letter

Although we actively encourage your guidance and participation with this activity, it may be that you are able to take a bit of a step back. In the activity book, Lucy and Sarah give your children the freedom to decide whether or not they want to complete the activity by themselves or with you. Whereas we felt that the last activity would be improved with your guidance, we feel that this activity should perhaps be led by the children. If they are having a little trouble getting started though, do remind them of when Sarah wanted to tell everyone how she was feeling but couldn't, and the advantages of writing it in a letter.

It has been created to facilitate the following three concepts:

♥ To allow children to accept feelings of all kinds.

We are finding more and more that society is labelling certain feelings as right or wrong, or good or bad. We believe that feelings are feelings, and that we should be given the freedom to not only express and explore, but most of all, to accept that the way we feel is OK. We believe this is especially important for children at significant phases in their emotional development. We do not mean that a child should be encouraged to remain constantly angry (we are not advocating violence of any kind – feeling angry is OK, but the way it is being expressed may not be). It is more about understanding that there is an emotional scale and having the freedom to drift up and down it. Sometimes your children may have felt belittled when they have expressed their feelings, so we are trying to prevent any child supressing these feelings due to fear. We have both experienced the long term effects that can have on a child.

♥ To teach children different methods of expressing their feelings.

Each child will have their own way of expressing how they are feeling. Some may be verbal, others may be physical, some may be secretive and others may need to talk about the same problem with numerous people. All of these are acceptable, but it is important for a child to learn how to effectively process their emotions and also how to become unstuck from a single emotion. You may be in a situation where your children don't fully comprehend what they are feeling. If this is the case, the focus just needs to be on release rather than an understanding or labelling of the feeling. We have an activity later on which will help cover this in more depth.

♥ To give children the space to express feelings that they may not want other people to know about.

You may need to have a conversation to reassure them that not everything they think and feel is for everyone to hear. Try not to worry if they choose to keep certain feelings to themselves, even if it feels a little hurtful. The important aspect is that they are encouraged to express how they are feeling either by talking it through with somebody else, writing it in a secret letter or speaking to animals. At this stage you are simply there to listen, not offer solutions. So, continue to remind your children that you are there if they need someone to talk to.

We also want your children to feel that even though they are a child, they are still entitled to some privacy. Furthermore, exploration of these mixed emotions will be particularly prevalent in the 'Tween' years. They will be going through the added trials of hormonal and physical changes, which will take time to settle.

<u>Trigger questions:</u>

♥ Have you got some extra feelings/thoughts that you would like to express today?
♥ How would you like to express them?

♥ Do you want to talk this through at the end or keep it to yourself?

Note: If you are concerned that your children are keeping something serious from you (such as bullying or abuse), and you do not feel it is in their best interests to keep it a secret, we suggest that you try to gently talk this through with them, at a pace that suits them. Try to use clear, direct language when asking the questions. You will not offend or shock them, but use of black and white words will be understood the best. It may take them a while to tell you the whole story but better to go through it steadily than force them to talk about something they are really battling with, all in one go. They are more likely to confide in you if you provide a non-judgemental, patient ear. If you do find yourself in this incredibly difficult situation, make sure you give yourself permission to ask for help too.

Activity 6: Acts of Kindness

We don't need to tell you that acting kindly towards others and receiving acts of kindness is a positive way to live. That is a given. We do feel however, that we need to introduce this concept to children. We would therefore like to explore kindness a little further in this activity. To save you flicking back through the pages, please see below the list of different ways you may show kindness/praise to children:

- They may like to be told in words what they have done well, or what you like about them/their behaviour;
- They may feel proud of visual praise, such as a certificate or trophy;
- They may love physical contact from you, like hugs and kisses;
- They may perhaps want to spend some time with you as a reward, either to engage in something they love to do, or just for the pleasure of being in your company;
- They may express happiness when you have offered to do something for them, such as help them tidy up or fix something that has broken;
- They may get great enjoyment from you organising a surprise for them;
- They may be motivated by gifts;
- Or, do you perhaps have a child who shies away from too much spotlight and praise?

Love and kindness go hand in hand. At this point, we would like you to just take a moment to look at your go-to ways of acting kindly/lovingly towards children. We have seen an increasing amount of pressure on parents, in particular, in today's society to work incredibly long hours AND be there at the end of the day as an effective parent. We have seen this lead to feelings of guilt – parents can sometimes feel that they are not spending enough time with their children or that their children aren't receiving enough of their love. Understandably, this can then lead to over-compensation and parents trying to find the quickest way to make up for this. Quite often, the immediate answer is to turn to gift-giving. This can lead to children becoming dependent on receiving material objects to feel loved. We are simply passing on an observation here – there is no judgement or criticism on our part and we urge you to observe your own actions without judgement or criticism either.

(We're certainly not suggesting that you never buy gifts for children. And you may even be the guardian of a child who genuinely feels the most loved when they receive a gift. Either way, try to choose a gift that has more personal meaning than monetary value and perhaps try to set aside time for an outing/meeting where you go and buy/choose the gift together).

Sorry – getting off track there slightly!

This activity has been created to facilitate the following three concepts:

♥   To teach children how to recognise and receive kindness.

We would like children to understand and recognise when someone has done something kind to them or for them. This activity ties in nicely with the gratitude exercise. This is a great opportunity for children to develop their sense of self-worth and identity, through love and not arrogance. This is also a really good opportunity for you to observe what your children consider to be an act of kindness, to help you understand how they might receive love best.

There may have been points in their life when they have accepted a gift or act of kindness but then broken it, sabotaged it or rejected it sometime later. Although they may not understand why, behaviour such as this does tend to stem from feelings of anger or frustration, and perhaps that they don't deserve to receive love. They may push away a hug, try to leave the room or tell you to shut up. That is how it may look on the outside. Try not to take this personally. Instead, try to remember that these actions may be fuelled by the underlying feeling of a lack of self-worth. Don't worry though – with everything that you already know and are learning about your children, you will be able to turn this around.

- ♥ To teach children how to show kindness to others.

We want to actively encourage children to express kindness to others through different means. They can choose any of the options (listed above), depending on who they are giving to. This part of the activity is designed to develop and nurture an awareness that you can give to someone else without expecting anything in return. We would also like to ensure that during this activity, with your guidance, your children are prevented from thinking that acts of kindness are bartering or creating a debt. An act of kindness is to give or receive something **unconditionally**. You may like to start a conversation about how it feels to receive kindness and to teach your children that they have the power to give that same feeling to someone else. We would like them to choose to carry out these acts of kindness, but in creative ways so that they don't automatically fall back on material generosity. We would like them to learn the value of also giving someone your time, your physical affection or simply a compliment. You may like to draw on the examples in Lucy and Sarah, such as Grandma Roberts and Ruth sharing kind words with Lucy.

- ♥ To give children space to plan an act of kindness that they would like to carry out in the future.

There are many times that a thought passes through our mind about something we'd like to do for somebody else. But life then carries on and the thought comes and goes. This section of the activity is all about helping your children develop the skill of honouring their word. It's about them creating their kindness plan and acting upon it, before that thought has chance to escape.

Trigger questions:

- ♥ What has someone done for you that you think is kind?
- ♥ What have you done for someone that you think is kind?

- ♥ How did it feel to receive that?
- ♥ How did it feel to give that?
- ♥ Is there someone you can think of that you could do something kind for?
- ♥ What is that something?

Activity 7: Fire Drill

As you know by now, this book is not all about the candy-floss and ice-cream of raising/guiding/educating a Tween! We are only too aware of the melt-downs and struggles you will have to go through, sometimes on a daily basis. First of all, well done! These struggles are a natural part of child development (particularly in the 'Tween' years), and we didn't want to write a book that shied away from the reality of that.

We spent many hours and cups of tea on this activity, discussing how best to help you with such a hot topic.

As already discussed, we want children to feel the range of emotions that come as part of being a human. However, we don't feel it's OK for them to be physically violent towards you or others, or use these behaviours to control their environment or people around them. This activity is therefore designed to assist your children with learning how to manage their own emotions and not become dependent on others to do so for them. We would like them to have not only the self-discipline, but also your support to acquire and nurture this skill.

This activity also takes out the need for punishment on your part. But this doesn't mean that there aren't or can't be natural consequences for a child's actions. For instance, if a child has an anger outburst and 'trashes' their surroundings, it is then their responsibility, once calm, to tidy/fix it. It's OK to do this with your help, but the underlying message should be that it is predominantly their job to restore it to how it was.

We are going to specifically share some of Naomi's thoughts here. These are based on years of working with children with challenging behaviours through the use of horse therapy. Naomi says: horses give instant, honest, non-judgemental, non-critical feedback for each behaviour the child displays. The child then learns which behaviours on their part create which results/reactions on the horse's part. But the child is still given the freedom to choose which behaviours they would like to carry out. The horse's reaction will be directly related to the behaviour. The horse won't hold grudges or dole out punishments. They will simply give feedback. This is what we are hoping you will be able to do with the use of this fire drill.

It has been created to facilitate the following three concepts:

♥   To create space for children to better understand their own feelings and emotions.

We have all been there – it has been a long day at work, you forgot to wish your friend happy birthday, you then got stuck in traffic and your battery levels are seriously on red. Hopefully, we have a few years of experience behind us and a little bit of wisdom, and we will be able to control our emotions after such a day. Well, we'd like to think so, anyway! Try to think about a similar day from a child's perspective. They do not yet have that skill (and that's OK), and they're also lacking the ability to directly label and understand their emotions. This activity won't solve this problem – only time and experience can do that. But we have created it to help you manage it. We want children to know it's OK to feel raw emotions and that they don't need to supress them. Don't underestimate the power that a particular experience can hold for a child, as what may seem small to you is most certainly a big deal for them.

♥   To allow children to create a set of steps to follow before their emotions get out of control.

We would like to help you to help your children understand their own emotions and reactions to the best of their ability. We feel that one of the best ways to facilitate this is to create a set of steps to follow before things get too out of hand. Once your fire drill is in place, you may like to practice it, say, once every two weeks. Try to do this at a time when everybody is calm and all is restful. This will go a little way to ensuring that there is some level of muscle memory in place, which will help dramatically. Just a quick note: it's not a problem if you can't get through to your little volcanoes when they are in the depths of despair or

169

tantrum-ville. You don't need to try and communicate or reason with them at this point. Your responsibility in these moments is to help them calm down by following the steps of your fire drill.

♥   To teach children that even though they may not be able to control their feelings all of the time, there is always somebody there to help.

This is a highly charged, confusing time for children, and not being able to express how they are feeling and why, can lead to a lot of frustration. We can sometimes be left baffled by the enormity of their emotions and the 'drama' with which they can be expressed. But try to remember that this is very 'real' to them and an inevitable part of growing up. Try not to belittle them or label their feelings as 'silly'. We want children to know that even if they are having a melt-down, they have people around them who can guide them through it, and who will still love them when they are out the other side. This activity will hopefully lessen the hopeless feelings and stop them pushing you away due to a misguided thought that you can't help them. Instead, we hope that they will actively seek your help and guidance, and allow you to be their anchor whilst they weather the inside-storm. Just the simple act of telling a child that it's OK and that you will get through it together is huge. A couple of key points: 1) try not to take the insults personally; 2) try not to worry about judgement from others; 3) don't feel you have failed if you haven't prevented the outbursts from happening – they are simply part of child development; 4) try to always practice self-compassion; 5) even in these melt-down moments, believe it or not, this is a child doing their best.

Trigger questions:

♥   Can you tell me when you feel like a Feeling-Fire is beginning to grow?
♥   How do you behave when this is happening?
♥   What makes you feel calmer?
♥   What's the first thing we can do when you are really angry/upset?

- ♥ What's the next thing we can do? (repeat until fire drill is complete)
- ♥ Can we practice this when you feel happy?

Don't forget to repeat this activity as your child grows older and their needs change.

Activity 8: Judgement Day

Sorry everybody! Here's another tricky conversation to have with your little ones! Bear with us. Nobody likes to admit to having been 'wrongly' judgemental. But, it is possible to reach a stage in life when you give yourself permission to be human and truly understand that the world isn't going to end just because you didn't act at your best. It's a stage when you know the sun will still rise tomorrow and the world will keep turning. It is a very freeing point to get to, and we're hoping both you and your children will discover that things become less of a big deal when you take the pressure off getting it all right, first time. This can also steer us away from passing the blame ball and not taking our share of responsibility. It just isn't possible to get everything 'right' all of the time, and what an amazing snippet of wisdom to pass onto children.

If you genuinely learn from each 'wrong' judgement though, and truly look at your own part in it, you are less likely to do it again. Especially if you have been kind and forgiving towards yourself. And the good thing about behaviour (well, your own anyway), is that you can be in control of it, even when you're dealing with the not so fun stuff. What you can't do however is control another's behaviour – not even your child's (nor should you try) – that's their job. But, you can guide, steer and influence, and you can do great things with this.

One word of warning though – don't underestimate the growing pains and discomfort that can come as part of taking this journey and evolving into the best version of you that you can be.

This activity has been designed to facilitate the following three concepts:

♥ To help children to see that it's OK if they have unfairly judged someone or a situation.

Although this activity is quite complex in terms of the conversations and lessons it may evoke, the message is fairly simple. We would like children to begin to accept that, fundamentally, we are all human and we are here to grow and live these lessons. We want children to explore the act of judging and how it can sometimes be based on assumption rather than truth. Please feel free to use the example of Lucy and Molly to stimulate a conversation here. Ask your child what they think about Lucy's judgement and whether or not she could perhaps have done something differently. This activity may be especially beneficial to you if you have noticed your children becoming stuck in certain related thought patterns and unable to progress.

♥ To help children practice the skill of not being too quick to make unfair judgements.

We have all experienced the act of judging a situation or person too quickly and drawing the 'wrong' conclusions about that situation or person. And you know what? That's OK. We have probably all experienced the flip-side of this too whereby a person has judged us too quickly. This activity has therefore been created to expand children's awareness of the two ends of this spectrum, and to deepen their understanding about why it's important to develop and practice fair-judgement. We would also like to increase children's awareness of when past experiences may be influencing current decisions about people/events. We feel it's important to base opinions on that which is in front of us in any given moment and not let negative assumptions from the past sway our thoughts.

♥ To create the space within which children can forgive themselves for unfair judgement but also acknowledge their part in it, and to accept responsibility.

A child's character will determine their reaction to such a situation. They may or may not move on quickly and easily. They may dismiss it immediately or harbour negative feelings for time to come. If your child is hanging on to any guilt or regret of any kind, try to steer them away from any harsh self-criticism by reminding them that their initial reaction was OK. You may like to use the example of how Lucy first reacted to Molly's Facebook Friends Request. Helping your children to accept their first reaction doesn't mean that they shouldn't also understand that they were part of the situation. Again, this might be quite a difficult conversation to have. But, we feel it's important to encourage children to work towards resolving the problem, to prevent them getting stuck in it. Try to be kind and patient with this one. These situations are even difficult to deal with as adults! But, we feel that if your child learns to talk through these problems now, they will experience less emotional turmoil later in life.

Trigger questions:

- ♥ Can you think of a time when you unfairly judged a person or experience?
- ♥ Can you think of a time when you were unfairly judged?
- ♥ Is there something someone has said that still upsets you?
- ♥ Is there something you have done that you want to say sorry for?
- ♥ Did you find out the truth about this person and experience?
- ♥ Was it very different to what you thought it was?
- ♥ What would you like to do about it?

N.B. Sadly, we are only too aware of certain dangers and threats that children must be aware of today. We therefore urge you to continue teaching your children how to 'judge' if a person or situation feels unsafe and/or threatening, and how best to react, to ensure their safety. This is, of course, paramount and we would like to stress here that we are NOT suggesting use of fair-judgement in such situations.

Activity 9: Weekly Routine

Phew!! Finally – here is a nice, simple activity for you. So…routines…some people will be more inclined to manage their lives like a timetable, whereas others will be more 'fly by the seat of your pants'. There is no right or wrong way to live life – it is very dependent on your personality type and, to a certain extent, the examples you were shown during childhood. Either way, we believe there is true value in time management of some form. We have all experienced the hours flying by as a child and then the years, as an adult. So, we would like to help pass on the skill of making the most of our time. None of us knows when the last grain of sand will fall.

You will be well aware, by now, of our views on active time management, voiced in both Lucy and Sarah, and the Activity Book. We truly believe that when someone takes daily (or weekly) action towards achievement, they will receive a golden nugget of satisfaction that they are moving towards what they want. We feel that these people are then less likely to become frustrated and stagnant, and more likely to keep up momentum. It's also a great chance to learn what is achievable.

Your role throughout this activity is not to determine how your child should spend their time. Instead, it's to help highlight to them which activities might be the most useful in terms of them getting to where they want to go. We are not talking about major commitments, but small steps. Even tidying up after themselves helps them in some way, even though they may strongly contest that!

This activity has been created to facilitate the following three concepts:

♥   To help children learn the concept of time management.

What we spend our time doing can ultimately create the life we want. We all have 24 hours in our day, but how we spend them can determine our future. This is fairly self-explanatory. From a child's perspective however, they won't have a say in their whole 24 hours. For example, they must sleep and go to school at certain times. But, we would like to introduce the idea that they can have some control over how they spend some of their time. For example, they may learn that they can have time to do two extra-curricular activities each week.

♥ To help children learn that if you don't start taking action towards your dream-future, things won't change.

This is an important skill to nurture in children as it teaches them how to be responsible for decision-making and not just to expect that their future is a given. Try to be aware of what your child currently values (whether it is something healthy or not) as this is the thing they will be most motivated to spend their time doing. You might need to steer them away from, say, watching T.V or playing on their phone. Instead, perhaps try to use some of this time to help them plan what they are going to do that weekend. This will also help you if you find that you are sometimes struggling for ideas when they are bored.

♥ To teach children how to have respect for their time, and use it wisely.

If, in the unlikely event, your child chooses to spend no time working towards their dreams, life will respond. We urge you to let that unfold as much as you can, without intervening, so that your child learns from life's natural consequences. In this case, it would unfortunately be their dreams not coming true. We know it's hard, but try not to make all the decisions for them. Instead, let them be inspired to want to seek activities. This is a balancing act, because obviously we don't want children to be stagnant, but, we also want them to learn that self-discipline is from within, not from others. It is something they have to be able to motivate themselves with. If your child is really struggling and you're feeling a little lost and frustrated, a fair compromise would be to offer your child 3 options for how to fill a particular time slot.

Trigger questions:

- What would you like to do today?
- What do you want to work towards?
- What would you like to plan for the weekend?
- Shall we sit down and create your dream time table?
- How much time do you think you need to do that activity/task (feel free to steer your child to more realistic assumptions here)?
- Which part of your timetable do you have to do (i.e. sleep, homework, eating, school)?
- How much dream time does that leave you?
- Is your dream time table achievable? (feel free to guide them with this also).

Activity 10: Mistakes? What Mistakes?

This activity follows a very similar path to that of the judgement activity, so we will try not to repeat ourselves too much. When doing this activity remind your little ones about the part in Lucy and Sarah, when Sarah 'fixes' what she feels was a mistake, and makes Lucy her own 'What-I-Want-To-Be-When-I-Grow-Up' box.

We feel that this activity creates more, worthy opportunities for you to continue and expand on the conversation about how it is OK to make mistakes. It will also further develop children's understanding of the notion: 'my action creates this reaction in life'.

It has been created to facilitate the following three concepts:

♥ To give children the space and permission to admit to mistakes and learn that it's OK to make them.

We give you full permission to sit on your hands whilst your little 'Tween' problem solves here. One of the essential aspects of making a mistake is having the confidence to admit that you behaved in a way that perhaps wasn't your best, and taking steps towards 'fixing' it. In order to facilitate your children's self-exploration with and development of this skill, it's important that you don't step in and do it for them. Instead, try to offer reassurance that even though it may take them a little while, they are doing absolutely fine.

♥ To create space for children to figure out their own techniques and ways of handling such situations.

Every child is different and this activity will pull out and highlight different traits and strengths in your child's character. You may even be surprised by what you discover. How your child chooses to 'fix' a mistake will depend somewhat on their personality, but also their comfort zone and what they feel they are allowed to do. For example, if your child prefers to apologise in a letter rather than face-to-face, give them the freedom to do so. It's much better that they learn to fix a mistake with confidence rather than not fix it at all because they are uncomfortable with the method.

♥ To create space for children to try and attempt, and to nurture their 'give it a go' attitude.

In this activity we are obviously focusing on children working out how to 'fix' a mistake and carry out the steps involved. But, we feel the lessons here can be carried over into all aspects of life.

If we continually step in for children, they will never have the opportunity to learn. It's so important to keep encouraging children to 'have a go'. While ever your child is attempting, they are succeeding. However, the moment they stop trying, they are, in a sense, failing. A child's 'try' is one of life's greatest gifts as, no matter what they choose to do when they grow up, they will always find a path to get themselves there. Alternatively, if a child loses their 'try', they are more likely to be controlled by outside events, and feel they have no power over this.

There is a growing tendency in society to make every single child feel that they have won, by giving out awards to everybody. We feel this is a completely unrealistic view of real life. A child who has been awarded for every action may then face great disappointment later on in life which they may find extremely difficult to process, due to a lack of opportunity to do so in their younger years. A child needs to experience contrast for them to be able to differentiate between what is success and non-success for them. As hard as it is to watch a child problem solve, especially if there is a time frame for the task to be completed, we feel it's important that you create space for them to experience this essential part of life.

Trigger questions:

- ♥ Do you feel you have made a mistake?
- ♥ What was it?
- ♥ Have you fixed it?
- ♥ If not, what do you think you could do to fix it?
- ♥ Do you want some help?
- ♥ How do you feel about making the mistake?
- ♥ Is there anything I can do to help you feel better?

N.B. Please feel free to use an alternative word to 'mistake' throughout this activity if you feel there is a more suitable one for you and your child/children.

Activity 11: Feel-Good Box

This activity is one of the more self-explanatory ones, on the surface, but we would like to offer a deeper explanation about which skills we are trying to help children develop. We all know that things run a little smoother when we are feeling happy. We seem able to handle the bumps in our journey with laughter rather than with rage, and we can bring out the best in ourselves and each other. Yet, when the chips are down, it can feel like the leap from despair to happiness is virtually impossible. We both recognise that there is an emotional ladder to be climbed at times like these. It isn't just a case of bouncing from the bottom rung of sadness straight up to the top one of relief. There is a process to go through and we hope to offer some tips on how to make that process just a little bit easier.

Often when we are down, people offer what they feel are words of wisdom and support. Of course, it's lovely when those around us try to lend a hand through the tough phases, but we may be told things like "don't worry about it", or "stop stressing and try not to think about it". That's all well and good, but sometimes in those moments, such words can fall on deaf ears. If only it were that simple. This is incredibly difficult advice to follow as an adult, let alone as a child.

So, we have designed this activity to encourage your children to create an actual physical place they can go to when they're feeling low. We have both learnt that movement can create momentum and this can move us out of the feelings we don't want to be feeling, and into those that we do.

It has been created to facilitate the following three concepts:

♥ To help children learn how to be selfish…the good kind!

First of all…being selfish can be a good thing! Do not think for a second that taking time out to nurture yourself and make yourself feel good, is not a worthy use of your time. It certainly isn't something we need to burden ourselves with guilt over. We will sing from the roof tops until the very end that being selfish is a valuable skill to have. If you take time to look after your own well-being, you are more likely to have love and kindness to offer to other people. If your child can learn from an early age how to de-stress, laugh, and take care of their physical and mental well-being, they are less likely to have health problems later on in life. Your children have to spend a lot of their time engaged in structured, compulsory commitments. We are hoping that this activity will afford them a little freedom to be master of their leisure time and to actively fill it with positive pursuits. We are hoping that they will hold onto the value of taking time to look after themselves, something we feel we should all keep practising.

♥   To help children learn how to be kind to themselves.

This follows roughly the same thread as learning how to be selfish. But it's a skill that can be so easily forgotten whilst we are running around looking after others or trying to please others. We can often forget to offer ourselves the same level of kindness. We are sometimes so critical of ourselves and treat ourselves in a way that we would never treat a friend. We are becoming increasingly aware of the new pressures on the current generation – pressures to fit in, to look a certain way, to tackle the world of social media (especially!) and to grow up too quickly. Anxiety, depression and low self-worth are becoming familiar words when we are talking about children…CHILDREN! We want so much for your children to learn how to be their own cheerleader and to develop a sound system of self-support. So, when they receive external criticism or experience a setback, they will be better equipped to deal with it. We're hoping that, with these new skills, such disappointments won't cripple them. We're hoping that they will take them and use them as a spring board to developing even further as an amazing human being!

- ♥ To help children learn that they have the power to turn things around, whenever they like.

It seems to have become a bit of a tradition to have a 'bad day' or even a 'bad week'. We seem increasingly unable to prevent the not so nice side of life completely overshadowing the nice side. Naturally, there are going to be good times and bad times. But, we'd like to help you teach your children how to move through a 'bad hour' but then, just as importantly, how to leave that hour behind. We would love them to learn how to move forwards into the next good hour without any shadows hanging over them. The box can help your children create the tools they need to be able to turn things around for themselves. It's a happy place for them to go to, filled with things that make them happy. It's also an opportunity for them to learn just what it is that makes them happy and what kind of things they need in order to move forwards from something upsetting or unpleasant. It's about creating happiness in a unique way – however that looks for each individual child. It's not all doom and gloom though – the box isn't just an escape for your children when they are feeling down. It is also there for when they just want to continue to feel good.

Trigger questions:

- ♥ What makes you feel happy?
- ♥ What would you like to put in your box?
- ♥ Do you need me to get anything for your box?
- ♥ Would you like any help?

Activity 12: Let's Get Outside!

Absolutely every parent/carer/guardian in the world is faced with daily reminders and challenges about how to get their children outside. It may seem like such a simple concept, but sometimes not so, as you try to prize the TV remote from their sticky fingers. We have both seen, first-hand, the benefits of getting children outside more. But, we know it isn't as straightforward as it sounds, so we wanted to give you as much guidance as possible.

We would also like children to be more actively involved in the decision to get outside, rather than viewing it as just another chore. T.V and computer games have become so ingrained in some children's lives that 'getting outside for some fresh air' almost feels like an endurance task.

We also recognise that you may be exhausted, and the last thing you want to do is run around the garden playing 873 games of tag. So, these activities have been designed to help children become more in charge of and engaged in their time outside. You will notice that there are numerous choices. This is simply so that there is hopefully an option for each child, no matter their character. You may be surprised by which one your child picks...or not.

The activity has been created to facilitate the following three concepts:

♥ Quite simply, to encourage children to get outside.

We are not going to insult you by explaining the benefits of being outside and exercising. There is enough research available to back this up. But, what we would like to highlight is that it isn't as big a chore as we perhaps once perceived it to be. We would like to re-introduce it as a natural way of life that doesn't need over-thinking or avoiding.

♥   To stimulate children's imaginations.

We're sure, at one time or another, you will have heard a well-meaning adult say something along the lines of "children have no imagination these days". Whether or not this is true, we would still like to help nurture the part of a child's imagination that is needed for creative play/tasks. Please don't think we are suggesting that your child should never be exposed to T.V or computer games. This is part of the society we live in today, and it has its place. We are simply advising moderation. You may even have a child who *needs* that type of outlet and stimulation with which to develop.

♥   To teach children that no matter which personality type they have, there is an outdoor activity for them.

The reason we have suggested such a variety of outdoor activities is to stimulate the imagination of ALL children. We want every child to feel that there is an option for them, and that no matter where their motivation lies, whether this be doing things alone, or in groups, or conducting research, there is something they can do outdoors. We feel that this is also a useful opportunity for you to learn a little bit more about your Tween and what makes them tick. Try not to steer or influence their choices in this activity though. They may hone in on one or may choose two or three. This is definitely an activity in which we would like you to encourage your child to take the lead. And we're hoping that whichever activity they choose, this will be the one that will bring out the best in them.

Trigger questions:

♥   Which activity do you most like the sound of?
♥   Who would you like to do it with?
♥   Do we need to get anything ready?
♥   Would you like any help?
♥   Would you like to do any of the other activities?

Activity 13: Animal Omens

Bear with us with this activity. You may think we're going to get all airy-fairy on you, but we're not…promise. Admittedly, this is probably one of our more 'out there' activities, but we couldn't not put it in. We are pretty sure that all of you, at one time or another, have suddenly become aware of, for example, always waking up at exactly the same time, night after night, or hearing a certain song on the radio again and again. This usually leaves most people thinking, "Hmmm, I wonder what that means?" Even for just a fleeting moment.

In this activity we aim to expand on that concept and stimulate the curiosity of children. We would like to help highlight the unfolding process or sequence of magical events which can occur in the run up to reaching a goal or dream. We feel it's a journey to be enjoyed. We like to see the signs and symbols that people see along the way as 'happy post-it notes': little reminders that you're on the right track and that you're doing just fine – a little pick-me-up to encourage you to keep putting one foot in front of the other.

It has been created to facilitate the following three concepts:

♥   To help children to become more observant.

This is a valuable skill within itself. It teaches children to actively notice the world around them. This can also be seen as a form a mindfulness – a word that you are probably only too aware of now. Being mindful is simply the act of focusing on something, for a period of time. One of the added benefits of this is that, for that period of time, you are not focusing on any worries. We also like to think of the great outdoors as nature's supreme TV channel.

♥ To teach children to ask themselves if there is anything they are feeling or experiencing which needs their attention.

As mentioned, these signs and symbols can be seen as post-it note reminders. There may be something troubling your child or something on their mind, which they would like to process. It's sometimes helpful to have these little prompts pop up every once in a while: nature's 'to-do' list, which can help to focus the mind. Once your child has decided which animals are going to be their omens and what they stand for, each sighting of that animal will help them to check in with themselves. These sightings also create a great opportunity for you to start a conversation with your child. You may like to see if they have anything they want to tell you or talk to you about. For example, if the robin is one of your child's animal omens, and they symbolise new beginnings, your conversation may start in the following way: "Hey, there's a robin. Isn't that your sign for new beginnings? Are you creating something new right now or do you have a new plan in mind?"

♥ To raise children's awareness of who/what we are sharing this planet with and how our actions may influence them.

This concept is fairly self-explanatory and one we feel you will be able to take the lead with, depending on the interest your child shows. Obviously, we are not alone on this planet and our actions do influence the space our children are growing up in and the space their children will grow up in. We don't have to look far these days though to find useful information about what we can do to support wildlife and what conservation organisations are doing to clean our oceans and restore our forests. Perhaps offer a little information to your child and then give them the space to ask and explore further if they like. This may even fuel another self-made activity.

Trigger questions:

♥ What are your 7 animals?

- ♥ What does each of the animals mean to you (please feel free to use our examples)?
- ♥ Can you think of any animals you have seen recently?
- ♥ Would you like to make a collage of your animals?

Activity 14: Seven Areas of Life

OK, it has to be said…this is our favourite activity! And, if there is only one activity that you choose to continue with for years to come, we fully encourage it to be this one.

The philosophy behind this activity is one that we have both infiltrated into our lives and lived by for a number of years now. We have found it to be hugely beneficial in terms of maintaining a sense of fulfilment. We are not saying that when tragedy strikes in one of the areas that it isn't the most heart breaking, consuming event. (Such as that experienced by Lucy and Sarah). We are simply offering this as a tool so that children can keep better track of how each area of their life is developing. It can also be used to prevent them becoming fixated on just one area. We don't believe that all areas are equally weighted though, or that all areas demand attention at all times. There are clearly going to be phases of life when children spend more time on just one or two specific areas.

Through use of this tool, your children will also begin to build an awareness of how the people around them choose to spend their time. We feel it's important for them to not only learn how to respect their own use of time, but that of others as well. What seems like an important area to us might not be to someone else, but this is to be respected, not resisted.

We are aware that your children will only just be at the very beginning of building an awareness of this philosophy/way of life. So, don't worry if there are a lot of questions and furrowed brows. This is a skill to be nurtured and developed at a pace that is right to the individual. But, one major advantage to living this way is that we don't hand over the full responsibility of our happiness to just one area. This may help to free you from the responsibility of trying to be your child's everything, and may also help them to independently seek a more balanced life.

It has been created to facilitate the following three concepts:

♥   To help teach children how to maintain balance.

As with a lot of our activities, we are not so concerned with your children understanding the philosophy behind it. We hope that completion of the activity will do the teaching! Learning how to break life down into boxes will help children start to manage the different areas. It's very easy for the boxes to become tangled together though, and to lose sight of which area perhaps needs some attention. Learning how to step back a little will also help to prevent your child fixating on just one area, which can lead to suffocation of that area. We would therefore like to help your children learn how to take action in more than one box. This tool will help your child to become a more rounded person, live a more fulfilling life and be able to seek enjoyment from different sources.

♥   To help children learn how to identify which life-area needs their attention.

Sometimes we can feel as if our whole life is going wrong and that everything is against us. Closer investigation can often reveal that it is, in fact, just one area that is causing problems. Having the tools and the ability to assess life in such a way will, not only help your child identify the problem area, but also maintain appreciation of the areas that are going well. This will help your child develop the skill of being able to put problems into perspective. This can prevent feelings of being overwhelmed and out of control, but can also open up the mental space for creating solutions.

♥   To teach children that the other areas of life can act as a support when one isn't going so well.

By ensuring that each area of your child's life is working efficiently, we hope that this will help to support you through the tough times and the challenges. The areas that are going well can serve as a much-needed 'pick-you-up' and give a moment of relief from what you are going through. This can also provide children with more confidence because if they receive a knock in one area of life, they will still have the strength from the other six to lean on. Whereas, if life is seen as a whole and you receive a knock, it can seem as if your entire world has come crumbling down. You may like to encourage your child to check in with this activity once a month or so, but it isn't something they need to be fixated on every single day.

Trigger questions:

- ♥ What are you going to write under each of your headings?
- ♥ Which areas are going really well?
- ♥ Is there an area that isn't going so well?
- ♥ Is there anything you can do to fix that now?
- ♥ Would you like me to help you with that?
- ♥ Is there an area that you have forgotten about?
- ♥ Would you like to do something about that?

Activity 15: Money, Money, Money

We're going to start the introduction to this activity with a favourite quote: 'manage your money instead of allowing your money to manage you!' We're becoming more and more passionate about raising children's awareness of the dreaded 'M' word. We seem to be meeting children who are unaware of what a 20 pence piece is, yet feel happy to ask for a £60 computer game. Money is going to be part of your child's life and a point of focus as they enter adulthood. However, in today's society, we are using new methods of payment such as Contactless and online banking. Unfortunately, this is going to lessen your child's interaction with actual money. We no longer count the pennies and pounds on the kitchen table. This may mean that when your child receives their first pay check or student loan, they may not have the understanding or knowledge of what to do with it or how to manage that money.

This activity is simple, but will help children when they reach the age where they will be handling their own money. It may also help prevent them getting into financial difficulties, and may also help them develop good financial habits and make sound financial decisions, which yield rewards.

We feel that you will need to step in and guide your child with this activity as they may not yet understand the reason for or purpose of each jar. They may also struggle in the beginning with how to divide their money. We would just like to say at this point, that this system works just as well with pennies as it does with pounds, so please don't feel that lessons can only be learnt with large quantities of money. It's all relative. We are not concerned at all with the amounts in each jar. We are hoping to nurture the skill of managing the amounts given, however much that is.

This is also a great opportunity for you to teach a second skill: that of earning. You may, for example, want to begin a 'Chores = Cash' system in your household/setting – perhaps 5p for bed-making/tidying, or £2 for car-cleaning. Have fun with this – there are no rules. But, this will help to build an understanding that in order to receive money you must provide a service or a product. You may even find you have a budding entrepreneur on your hands! If so, let them fly! They will learn a great deal by, for example, selling biscuits to neighbours or cutting grass for different families. All we advise is that you're always there, just in the background, to monitor those slightly crazier schemes!

This activity has been created to facilitate the following three concepts:

♥   To help children understand the role of money in life.

Whether we have a little or a lot, and whether we like it or not, money has a role to play in life. It can bring great enjoyment or great frustration, sometimes in equal amounts. It is almost impossible to not attach in some way to money and the part it plays in your life. We are hoping that this activity will at least raise children's awareness that money does need managing, but, that it doesn't need to control you and that it can actually assist you.

♥   To teach children the life skill of delaying gratification.

There is no doubt about it – we live in an instant society. We can have anything we want at the click of a button and we can sometimes expect money to just instantly appear so that we can purchase the thing we want, now. We can have an instant holiday and pay it off later, or buy something we don't have the money for. Sometimes this is necessary in life, but we would like to help children understand and get into the habit of saving. The step-by-step process that your child will go through of putting money into a jar; adding to it each week; and then buying the product once they have saved enough, will clearly demonstrate to them that there is sometimes a journey to be taken to get what you would like. Working and saving for something may also lead to a deep sense of pride and a different sense of enjoyment, than if a child had simply received something they hadn't had to work for.

♥ To teach children how to divide and manage their money.

This one is fairly self-explanatory but may need your assistance. There are two ways to spend money: the first is to divide it up and save for different things, and the second is to blow it all in one go, on one big thing. Your child will likely fall into one of the two categories. We feel this is OK – there is no right or wrong way to do it. But, we would like this activity to provide them with a clear choice of how they would like to manage it, and awareness of the consequences of those choices.

Trigger questions:

♥ How much is this? (to be asked as you hold up different pieces of money);
♥ What is 25% of this amount?
♥ What would you like to save for?
♥ How much will that cost?
♥ How long will it take you to save that?
♥ Do you think you would be happy to wait to see if that item goes on sale?
♥ What could we do to help you earn that?
♥ Is there anything you want to buy now?

Activity 16: Pay It Forward

So, have you been asked for a big role of bin liners yet?! Is your Tween dashing around their room, flinging clothes here and there and making piles of unwanted items? Or, have they been making a plan with you to do so? If so, we would like to say…sorry! We're hoping it won't look like a bomb site for ever. Joking aside though, we feel that this activity is hugely helpful, on so many different levels. We live in a very disposable world, where it is incredibly easy to accumulate lots of 'stuff'! But, we also live in a world where, generally speaking, we're also concerned with recycling. So, this activity acknowledges what we, as individuals, can do to help. This enjoyable activity will not only benefit your Tween, but will also help a wider group of people. Imagine throwing a pebble into a pond and watching the ripples spread wider and wider. We like to call it, 'spreading the love'!

It has been created to facilitate the following three concepts:

♥ To teach children about a particular type of kindness and 'paying it forward'.

Imagine this scenario for a second…your child has spent some time in their room putting thought into which items they no longer need or want. By our calculations, that's at least an hour they haven't been on their phone or in front of the T.V… What a magical bonus! They have not only focused their attention on a meaningful task, but have also created space in their environment to receive something new. This is also a fantastic time for children to begin to understand that their actions can influence a great number of people. For example, the simple act of donating something helps: your child; the organisation; and the person who will ultimately buy their unwanted item. This is a really relaxed, practical way to demonstrate generosity, without the pressure to perform an act of kindness. As a guardian/parent, we hope that you will be able to either plan, or help to plan, an outing for your Tween, to visit their chosen charity shop, and perhaps the nearest coffee shop to grab a piece of cake to celebrate!

♥ To teach children how to let go of possessions and allow that space to be filled with something else.

Letting go is not always the easiest task to carry out. We have all stood in front of our wardrobes staring at that top or those jeans we haven't worn in 5 years, thinking, "I'll hang onto them a little longer, just in case." But, we feel it can actually be very liberating when you can get to the point where you give yourself permission to let go of those jeans, metaphorically speaking. At that moment, you are in a state of acceptance that you have moved on from a certain stage in your life, and are ready to enter a new phase. You are allowing yourself to transform parts of you and your life. One thing is guaranteed, people do not stay the same. We change, we evolve, we learn, we explore and we grow. It's important to know how to let go of the old and welcome in the new. We feel this is a valuable skill to pass on to children. You may need to guide your child through this and step in here and there. We wish you luck as you embark on the conversation about letting go of that piece of Lego or the Barbie with one leg missing! (Please have a look through the trigger questions below. It can sometimes be easier to let go of something when you know it has a greater purpose).

♥ To educate children about different charitable organisations and what they are for.

Whilst you are tucking into your tea and cake after that visit to the charity shop with your child, or hearing all about it afterwards, we feel this is a great opportunity to start a conversation about different organisations, how we can help and support, but also for you to find out what it is that your little one is passionate about. It may be animals, people (old, young, those with disabilities), natural disasters, health or homelessness. This is also quality time for you and your child, as today, you have something in common to talk about and that you are both interested in.

Trigger questions:

- ♥ What do you want to donate to charity?
- ♥ Can I double-check your bag please?
- ♥ Which organisation would you like to donate to?
- ♥ Why do you like that organisation?
- ♥ Are you sure about donating that item? This is an item I have seen you use/play with recently;
- ♥ What about this item? I haven't seen you use it/play with it in a long time;
- ♥ What dream do you think your donation will help someone else achieve?

Activity 17: Selfie Video

Now, we all know that Selfie-Photos and Selfie-Videos are the latest craze. So, we thought we would put this to good use. We know from direct experience that this activity can be incredibly powerful! It can be incredibly empowering to see yourself and hear yourself as the person you want to be. We recognise that the term 'affirmations' can be taken to mean different things, due to the varying opinions surrounding it. The way we see it though, is that if you want to, for example, find a new job, you have to do something concrete each day to get there, such as organise interviews. But, first of all you have to confidently see yourself as a person who can and will attend interviews, and who is ready for a new challenge. Before we make big changes in our lives we usually run through a dialogue, either with ourselves or with friends/family. We like to talk through the changes we want to make, what we have to do to get there and who we need to be. This activity encompasses that – it's just that the video is doing the work for the children, and it can serve as a daily reminder of this inner dialogue. We are all aware of the process of change, but that sometimes the initial inspiration and excitement can often wane as we become distracted by life. We may find that we are not quite so focused on looking for those job vacancies, or that we are procrastinating about setting up another interview. We therefore hope that this video will help to keep your child on track.

It has been created to facilitate the following three concepts:

♥ To help children see themselves as the person they want to be.

This activity is a light-hearted way of playing pretend. We hope that children will see that it can be fun to dream and that dreams are achievable. Why not dream big? We are all humans at the end of the day, and we would like them to realise that they don't have to physically become a new person, but that they can achieve their dreams as the person they are today. In order for your child to reach their dreams, we feel that the two main elements that need to change are: their belief in themselves and; the way they spend their practical time. We want your children to truly grasp that their dream is within their reach and that it isn't something reserved for another child.

♥ To help children become their own role-model.

It's wonderful to admire somebody who has already achieved what you want to achieve. But, we would like one of your child's role-models to be themselves! This will help your child to build their self-worth and their self-esteem. They will have the opportunity to take a step out of themselves, look in the mirror at their reflection, and say "I love that person", "I like being her/him" and "I am really proud of the person I am becoming". What could be better than that?

♥ To teach children the importance of creating time every day to focus.

This is self-explanatory and a concept that we have covered in many of the activities so far. It draws on one of our favourite notions – if you put time and effort into something, it will grow. If you need a bit of guidance with this one, flip back to the Dreaming Activity.

Trigger questions:

- ♥ What are your seven statements?
- ♥ Would you like help recording it?
- ♥ Who are you being while you record the video?
- ♥ Do you want to get dressed up for it?
- ♥ Shall we have a practice run through?
- ♥ Where would you like to record your video?

Activity 18: Letter from the Future

And here we have it…another way to dream! What a surprise! But, this activity allows your child to leap forwards into a future where their dream has come true. It provides children with an opportunity to look at the journey ahead, to see the ups and downs they could potentially encounter along the way, but not be afraid of them. It also gives them a period of time when they can fully explore their imagination with no fear of failure. To fully immerse yourself in this mind-set can also boost confidence levels and motivation. It may be that your child is feeling a little uncertain at the moment. If so, let them delve into this activity with total freedom.

It has been created to facilitate the following three concepts:

♥ To give children another tool which can be used to sharpen their focus.

This activity can be used by your child to help them focus on what it is they want to have in their life, and the direction they want their life path to go in. There are no rules with this activity.

♥ To teach children the wonderful art of patience.

As mentioned before, we live in a world of instant gratification at the moment. We can immediately have what we want at the click of a button, and don't have to wait in a way that previous generations did. We feel that this has its place in the world today. But, we also feel that it is hindering our ability to be patient. Patience is such a valuable life skill nowadays. We don't want your children to give up or lose hope just because they haven't seen results straight away. We want them to understand that there is a process and that sometimes it takes time to 'grow' the best dreams. Nobody has all of the knowledge they need straight away. There are pieces of information that we will pick up along the way, when we are ready to receive them. Receiving all the required information in the beginning could overwhelm us, and the majority of it would also be out of context and therefore, difficult to decipher. It's OK to focus on the destination, but we feel it is important that your child focuses only on that which needs to be done today. Completion of the immediate tasks will keep them moving.

♥ To give children hope and belief that their dreams will come true in time.

We all encounter disappointments and low points – they are inevitable. It's possible your child will doubt themselves and may even want to give up at times. But, we hope that reading their own words of encouragement, will refuel their hope and belief. We would like to keep the passion inside of them alive, and to encourage them to keep moving forwards. It can also be fun to re-read the letter once the dream has been achieved. Your child may realise that the journey wasn't quite what they expected it to be. There may have been setbacks where they thought they would have successes, and vice versa. But they will see that all of it is OK, and that a rocky road is no reason not to travel the road. There is no such thing as a perfect journey.

Trigger questions:

♥ Would you like to sit down and write your letter?
♥ Which dream would you like to write about?
♥ What year is the future letter being sent from?
♥ Would you like to do it by yourself or would you like some help?

Activity 19: New You – New Environment

This may seem obvious, but we have encountered the following scenario countless times: people working so hard to make improvements on themselves, only to step back through their front door and their old environment, and being pulled back to the person they are trying to leave behind. The skill we are aiming to equip children with through this activity may not be fully understood until adulthood. But, if they can get into the habit of actively seeking and welcoming a change in their environment now, the big changes later in life may not feel quite so dramatic and overwhelming.

If you want to become vegetarian you need to replace your meat-related books with vegetarian cook books. If you want to be a writer you need to create space to write. Our external environment doesn't have to be permanent. And we want your children to understand that they have the power to transform it into what they need and want, to thrive.

It has been created to facilitate the following three concepts:

♥ To teach children that it can be easier to be a new person if you alter your environment.

Our external world is constantly changing. There are areas of it we can't control, for example, society and nature. However, there are the more immediate environments that we feel your child can influence and change, for example, their bedrooms and wardrobes. We would love your child to learn the skill of personal transformation, initially, in these safe environments. With your guidance, they will discover that it is absolutely OK for things to change and evolve, and that they can have a say in what and who they change into.

♥ To teach children that it can be fun for their external world to reflect the changes in their internal world.

We have covered many serious activities throughout the book which involve a lot of thinking, planning and creative work. We apologise! But, this activity is a chance to just have fun. Let your child play, move things around, flick through magazines, explore colour and design some ideas. Just be honest and fair with them about their budget and limitations. You may even be able to use this activity alongside the Money Money Money activity to set up a savings plan with them.

♥ To give children time to be creative.

Your child may just be entering the phase where they are starting to have preferences for designs, colours, themes, and may be spending more time in their bedrooms with the door closed. Hopefully by now, at this stage in the activity book, both you and your child will have a much clearer idea about what their dreams are, and how to talk about them. Therefore, they will likely have some clear, creative ideas about what they would like to do with their personal space.

Try to give as much freedom as you can. If they want bright orange walls and you don't, perhaps you can agree on just one orange wall. This is an opportunity for you to give them the space to be whoever they want to be.

Trigger questions:

♥ What changes would you like to make to your bedroom?
♥ What colours do you really like at the moment?
♥ Do we need to go shopping?
♥ Is there any furniture you would like to change?
♥ Can we make any of the changes by painting old items, shopping in charity shops or re-vamping an existing item?
♥ Do we need to set up a money jar to pay for anything?

Activity 20: Secret Activity
Become the Guardian of Your Child's Worries

Our final activity. This activity is to be used carefully and wisely. It is not one to be used every single day as it can lose its effect. It has been created for you to use when there is something really troubling your Tween. It doesn't matter what it is – it may be something that we think is small, but for them, is catastrophic. You may notice that even after completing some of the relevant activities, your child just doesn't seem able to let go of it.

This is where you step in…

There are two ways that you can help your child let go of a worry. You can use the one that appeals to you the most, or you can use them both together.

Cord Cutting:

1. Get a piece of string, scissors, paper, pen, cardboard box and some Sellotape;
2. Ask your child to write their worry on a piece of paper and place it in the cardboard box;
3. Attach a piece of string to the cardboard box;
4. Ask your child to pull the cardboard box around the house/room (you can put something inside to weigh it down if you like);
5. Then ask them how this worry feels? Is it getting in their way? Is it holding them back? Is it preventing them from walking through doorways?
6. Pass the scissors to your child and say, "When you are ready, I want you to cut the cord (string) which connects to the worry, and let it go."

7. Your child should now cut the string but KEEP WALKING;

8. When they have walked to another part of the house, ask them, "How does it feel to no longer be dragging that worry around?"

   "Look back to see where you have left that worry."

9. LISTEN TO THEIR RESPONSE, SMILE, CLAP and CELEBRATE your child letting it go;

10. You should then collect the box and put it away, out of sight.

Bag of Worries:

This activity is useful whether you have a talkative Tween or a more private one. Either way, you will know if something is troubling them. Set aside some extra time at bedtime or during the day, when you can sit with them and talk about the thing that is troubling them. You will need paper, a pen and a bag of some sort.

Don't push your child to reveal everything if they feel reluctant. But try to encourage them to share at least some of their worries. Try to ask open-ended questions so that you are not steering the conversation. Try not to 'fix' it in these moments or offer advice. This is just an opportunity for your child to offload. At this point, write the name of the worry on a piece of paper, fold it up and put it in the bag. Tell them that for tonight, at least, you will be guardian of that worry, and that they don't need to think about it anymore whilst they sleep.

Conclusion

Congratulations!!! You made it!

You have taken on one of the hardest jobs in the world – that of parent/carer/guardian. The hours you put into your child, the effort, the thought and most of all, the love – there is no other job that asks for such a commitment.

This book is yours now, to be used time and time again. And you never know, maybe your children will use it with their children, and reminisce about the activities they did with you. Certain activities may get lost and forgotten. Others may become treasured for life.

Memories are our greatest gifts, and what you have just done is create so many beautiful ones. It won't always have been an easy journey, but your child can hold onto these lessons and memories for the rest of their life. That legacy is worth its weight in gold, and you are incredible for being part of it.

We have just one hope – that you will witness even one small positive change in your child, one small positive change in you, and one small positive change in your relationship together.

It has been our absolute pleasure to create this for you.

We both wish you so much love and luck in both your and your child's future, as you continue on this EPIC journey called life.

Naomi and Samantha